The
Personal Power
Formula

The
Personal Power
Formula

A Practical Guide to
Self-Discipline and Personal Growth

GARY G. TAYLOR, Ph.D.

Library of Congress Catalog Card Number: 82-72272
ISBN 0-88494-459-X

First Printing, 1982

Lithographed in the United States of America
PUBLISHERS PRESS
Salt Lake City, Utah

Contents

Chapter 1

Personal Power Perspective

Alice squirmed on the bench during sacrament meeting. A size sixteen figure in a size fourteen dress is always uncomfortable, especially when the wearer is listening to a sermon on self-improvement. Moved by the emotion of the moment, and aided by her temporary distance from temptation, Alice resolved to get control over her weight problem once and for all. "No more sweets, and I'm going to start exercising every day!" she vowed.

Alice maintained her self-commitment for about three hours. At that point, the smell of her daughter's freshly baked chocolate chip cookies was too much to handle. After breaking her promise by eating a few cookies, Alice slipped into a loose-fitting dress and, in the words of her children, "pigged out." Almost needless to say, her other good intention with respect to exercise suffered a similar fate.

Gerald was in the same sacrament meeting. Though most of the ward members didn't know it, Gerald had a bad temper. He too was moved by the spirit of the meeting to improve himself. Gerald pledged to himself and to his wife, Grace, that he would overcome his problem.

Unfortunately, the meeting did not motivate Grace to work on her nagging and complaining approach to her husband. On the way home, Grace complained about Gerald's driving too fast, about his being altogether too friendly with Sister Johnson, and about the fact that the lawn hadn't been mowed for a week. Gerald bit his tongue and didn't respond to the anger welling up inside. A later criticism proved to be too much, however, and Gerald found himself again fuming and swearing at his wife.

Bishop Harris was another person moved by the spirit of the sacrament meeting. His assignment as ward leader demanded a lot of time, but the bishop felt a strong need to work on his personal journal. "I'm going to do it," he said to himself during the closing hymn, and he felt the sweet influence of the Spirit validate his decision.

That evening Bishop Harris arranged to spend a few minutes on his journal, but found himself instead on the telephone with a ward member in distress. The next few days went about the same way. Something invariably came up whenever he was about to get to the project. Soon his resolve disappeared, and his journal was left undone.

These three individuals are like many of us. Often we will think of doing something that would be good for us, but we don't do it. Or, conversely, we recognize the damage inherent in particular behaviors but persist in them anyway. Sometimes our environment presents us with too many temptations (as with Alice and the chocolate chip cookies). Anger can get in our way (as did Gerald's anger toward his nagging wife), or sometimes our busy schedules interfere with goal achievement (as in Bishop Harris's case). Many other obstacles can also come between us and attainment of our goals. In fact, multiple factors are usually involved whenever we have difficulty reaching our objectives. For example, along with the factors identified in the three illustrations above, low self-esteem, unrealistic expectations, and insufficient commitment were also involved.

This book identifies some of the obstacles that get in the way of self-development and provides practical suggestions regarding how to increase our power to improve ourselves. This *personal power formula* is derived from the scriptures, from psychological literature, and from the personal experiences of hundreds of people who have learned to take charge of their lives.

Taking Charge of Your Life Means . . .

Before going on, answer yes or no to the following questions to determine the extent to which you currently exercise power over yourself. (You may also wish to have someone close to you answer these questions in terms of how he rates your personal power. Then compare evaluations and discuss the implications of any similarities or differences observed.)

1. Am I free of unwanted habits (e.g., smoking, drug/alcohol use, overeating, procrastination, temper)?
2. Do I maintain a regular exercise program?
3. Is my weight within desired limits?
4. Do I always control my temper?
5. Am I in control of my emotions?
6. Am I open with my feelings with those I care about?
7. Am I assertive without being unkind or manipulative?
8. Do I consistently maintain a close relationship with the Lord?
9. Do I regularly delay immediate pleasure for long-term rewards?
10. Am I honest about myself with others, even when the truth is uncomfortable?
11. Do I keep information secret that is given me in confidence?
12. Do I avoid accepting or transmitting gossip?
13. Is my life balanced effectively between personal, family, church, and relationship needs?
14. Do I set and reach my goals effectively?
15. Do I say no when I feel I should?
16. Do I have energy sufficient to complete my daily plans?
17. Do I get sufficient rest and recreation?
18. Are my mood and outlook positive?
19. Am I friendly?

20. Am I free of fear and worry?
21. Do I accept the things that can't be changed about myself, others, and my environment without bitterness and complaint?
22. Am I at peace with the unknown?
23. Is my behavior typically natural, simple, and often spontaneous?
24. Am I problem-centered (focused on problems outside of myself) as opposed to being ego-centered (focused on problems within myself)?
25. Do I have a good sense of humor, but never at the expense of someone else?
26. *Have I answered all of these questions honestly, without hedging?*

If you answered yes to all of the above questions, hang on; you are seconds away from being translated! Developing personal power is a lifelong pursuit for all of us. Stated another way, even exceptionally strong people have power failures occasionally. Weak people can obviously become stronger, but strong people can become stronger, too. The exciting thing is that whenever a person has a full charge of personal power, his life can begin to work especially well.

Again, this book is designed to offer suggestions to help *you* gain maximum power over yourself, but it can also assist you in helping others to gain personal power. At times, family members, friends, or those you counsel with in your Church assignments will likely seek help with self-development issues. Ideas in the chapters that follow should be of value in such situations.

Remember Perspective

Before going on, you might take a moment to remember that perfection is a one-step-at-a-time process, and you seriously undermine your progress when you expect too much too soon. Developing total self-discipline is similar to mastering any other complex task—it takes practice, trial and error, mistakes along the way, *and a lot of time.* How quickly a person develops this skill is not nearly as important as is the need for him to continue trying. This was discussed previously in *The Art of Effective Living* (Gary G. Taylor, Salt Lake City: Bookcraft, Inc., 1980).

It is also important to remember that this book pertains to *self* and not to *other* direction. Attempting to manipulate or control others causes nothing but trouble for everyone concerned— largely because it violates the principle of free agency. Others likewise cannot control us. Rather than blame parents, spouses, employers, or any other persons or circumstances in the world, we must assume final responsibility for both our feelings and behavior.

How Can This Book Help?

Many Latter-day Saint authors have discussed the need for self-direction, but few have focused on the question of how to get the job done. The intent in what follows is to provide practical suggestions regarding how to improve our self-development ability. Each of several critical elements in personal power is described, along with techniques for improving our situations with respect to each element. Step-by-step plans for solving particular personal power problems are also given. Before getting to specifics, however, chapter 2 focuses on the importance of gaining mastery over self and on some of the general issues involved in self-direction.

Personal Power
Is Essential

A friend of mine has a sign on his desk saying, "If it feels good, do it!" The problem with that philosophy, of course, is that feeling good, at least in the long run, often requires *not* doing it. Or it requires that we do painful things occasionally. In fact, lasting happiness is available only to those who become effective at self-direction. The following examples illustrate some of the reasons why personal power is so essential to happiness.

Peace of Mind Through Power Over Self

Karen was active in the Church—she paid tithing and attended meetings—but she was also involved in drugs and adultery. On the surface Karen claimed to be at peace. She appeared to be happy in spite of the obvious contradictions in her life, and at first glance she seemed to have little guilt over her split loyalties. As her psychologist, I was beginning to think that Karen was the first exception that I had ever seen to the rule "No man can serve two masters" (3 Nephi 13:24). During her third professional visit, however, she began to get in touch with feelings that she had seldom admitted, even to herself. With sobs of deep despair she expressed feelings of self-doubt, suicidal thoughts, and great emotional distress. I have seen many people in emotional pain, but none suffered more than Karen at that moment.

Karen's example indicates how difficult it is to have peace of mind without having congruence between what you believe and what you actually do. Effective self-direction gives you the power to keep beliefs and behavior in harmony.

Personal power also helps free people from worry in general. How many people do you know who disturb themselves with excessive worrying? It's unfortunate that many suffer emotional distress and ill health because they constantly worry about what might (but hardly ever does) happen. From an objective vantage point, it's obvious that such individuals are often hurt as much from worrying about what *might* happen as they would be if the imagined calamities actually occurred.

Personal power allows us to effectively handle difficulties, but also gives us the faith not to worry excessively about issues beyond our control.

Power for Better Interpersonal Relations

Edward has few friends. He claims to be happy with his life as a loner, but his countenance and behavior betray him. He just doesn't look happy. He often wears a frown and his face has a tight, drawn look to it. Even when he smiles, the effort seems forced and unfelt. Edward claims that no one reaches out to him at church or elsewhere, which is generally true. Actually, a few do try, but unfortunately Edward leaves quickly after meetings and his negative, distant demeanor discourages people from reaching out to him.

Edward needs more personal power to be effective socially. Introducing yourself to others, participating effectively in group activities, and cultivating close friendships all require self-confidence and self-discipline. Since no one is perfect, social exchange also requires you to have the ability to handle offense from others and disappointment when people let you down.

George has a problem similar to Edward's, but for a different reason. George has few friends because his loud, forceful style tends to frighten people off. He talks so much that many people actually turn the other way when they see George coming. They fear getting caught in a long and essentially one-sided conversation about some topic of little interest to them. (Usually the topic is George.)

Power over self allows you to be yourself in relationships. Obviously, those with control over their feelings and behavior don't dominate discussions or insist on having their way. They don't exhibit obnoxious, critical behavior (which is usually designed to keep others at a distance, or to build oneself at the expense of another). Backslapping and artificial enthusiasm are likewise unnecessary.

When a person is operating at full personal power, he is often labeled as being spontaneous, positive, fun, sensitive, helpful, a good listener, and easygoing. In other words, he becomes the kind of person that others enjoy.

Personal Power Frees Us From Unwanted Emotion

Sally has a problem with her temper, but, returning home from a highly motivating women's conference, she was convinced that she could control her emotions with her family. However, the scene that greeted her at home did her in. She sensed trouble immediately when she opened the door to the sounds of a football game on television in the family room and a fight over a toy in the living room (where children are not supposed to play). The kitchen counters were covered with jam, and the kitchen floor, freshly mopped before she left, looked like the floor at the local movie theater. Obviously Frank had been more interested in football than in watching the kids. Predictably, Sally came unglued at that point, tearing into her husband and children with words and actions that she later regretted. She certainly had reason to be angry and disappointed, but her reaction didn't help either herself or the situation.

Gaining power over emotions is one of the most important, but at the same time, one of the most difficult aspects of self-direction to master. Yet it is critical, for how we feel has a direct influence over both our happiness and our productivity. Counterproductive emotion is obviously painful, and unwanted fear, anger, and guilt undermine motivation and stand in the way of goal attainment.

With personal power, an individual will have a full range of emotional experience (emotional monotones are no fun), but that experience will be productive. Anger will encourage effective problem confrontation rather than lead to destructive behavior or bitterness. Guilt will lead to repentance rather than to self-hate. Fear will help create motivation for good works rather than immobilization or flight from reality.

Self-Direction to More Productivity

Sam is what most people would call a successful human being. He is law-abiding, honest with others, moral, a committed family man, and a consistent, hard-working employee. He accepts callings in the Church and serves effectively as long as the assignments involve behind-the-scenes responsibility.

Yes, Sam is successful, but he is functioning considerably below his peak level of productivity. Sam has never sought promotion in his work, although he is certainly capable of handling a more challenging position. Sam spends most of his spare time working with wood in his garage or watching television. He doesn't risk getting close to others, including those in his own family. Sam doesn't do volunteer work or in other ways involve himself in his community. He isn't social enough to be an effective missionary or home teacher, and he holds back from leading out in family activities. In these and in other ways, Sam is falling short of his potential.

Sam says he just isn't interested in doing any of these things, though they would benefit both him and those he loves. Actually, Sam is afraid to try. Fear, not disinterest, is the real problem. He needs a greater charge of personal power. If he had more faith in himself and greater self-discipline, Sam would set challenging goals for himself and he would have the self-direction ability to achieve them.

Sam assumes that others who are more productive than he is either have more talent or they are luckier. Usually, neither assumption is correct. Through faith in ourselves and in God, we can uncover hidden talents or create new ones. With personal power we also create "lucky" circumstances through an effective social network and a heightened awareness of opportunities.

Exaltation Requires Personal Power

It is obvious that self-mastery is extremely important in helping us live happy, productive lives in the here and now. But personal power is also a key to eternal life. No one can be exalted without the power and intercession of Christ—and no one will qualify for the intercession of Christ without the personal power to live his commandments. Brigham Young expressed this thought in the following manner: "But unless you control the passions that pertain to fallen nature—make all your faculties subservient to the principles God has revealed, you will never arrive at that state of happiness, glory, joy, peace, and eternal felicity that you are anticipating" (*Journal of Discourses* 8:116).

Power over self is a necessary prerequisite to exaltation for at least two reasons. First, only those who have demonstrated an ability to direct themselves will share an environment with God. The celestial kingdom wouldn't be the celestial kingdom if its inhabitants had to worry about neighbors ignoring their rights. Nor would it be a comfortable place if individuals there were not self-motivated and able to take care of themselves. Happily, no one will enjoy that society who has not learned to absolutely respect the rights of others and to contribute meaningfully to the common good.

Second, exaltation means sharing in the power of God. Fortunately, the omnipotence of the Father will be shared only with those who have learned to use power righteously. Can you imagine the result of giving the power of God to someone unable to control his emotions or behavior? By mastering ourselves, by overcoming unrighteous desires, by learning to operate only on the basis of righteous principles, we become eligible for greater responsibility and greater power.

Why Is It So Hard?

The advantages of personal power, from peace of mind in this life to exaltation in the life to come, are so fundamentally important to us that they become the very object of our existence. Yet personal power isn't so easy to come by. In addition to pointing out how important it is that we learn to direct ourselves, Brigham Young also indicated how hard the job is: "Now brethren, can we fight against and subdue ourselves? That is the greatest difficulty we ever encountered, and the most arduous warfare we ever engaged in" (*Journal of Discourses* 6:315).

Any mortal knows that Brigham wasn't overstating the point. It *is* difficult to gain self-mastery, but why? Perhaps one part of the answer lies in the fact that this is a new experience for us. In mortality, we find ourselves in strange bodies, feeling strange things, and absent from the direct, sustaining influence of the Father. Then, too, we have a common enemy who is anxious to frustrate our attempts to learn to operate in these bodies successfully. Lucifer and his allies are always ready to suggest attitudes and conclusions that will poison our systems and interfere with our ability to manage ourselves. "For he seeketh that all men might be miserable like unto himself" (2 Nephi 2:27).

Even without help from Lucifer, once in our bodies we tend to be short-sighted hedonists. The infant cries out for satisfaction of his needs with very little ability to delay gratification without upset. Many adults are almost as impatient. It is natural (but often counterproductive) to seek immediate reward even if it comes at the expense of longer term benefits. This is the case when we consistently put off pressing work in favor of play. It is also the case when we lie in order to avoid embarrassment from the truth—or when we do any of thousands of other things that are more comfortable at the moment, but that have long-term disadvantages.

Yes, it is difficult to master ourselves. But it is possible if we apply correct principles and persevere. We need to remember, however, that it takes more than resolve; self-direction requires skill. Fortunately, it is a skill that can be learned.

The Skill of Developing Personal Power

Perhaps one of the most common but unproductive beliefs about self-direction is the assumption that it depends on a personal attribute of will. Under this assumption, a person's will power determines his ability to direct himself. Unfortunately, this definition is circular and doesn't help clarify the concept. Suppose that you decide not to gossip, and you never again succumb to that temptation. How did you do it? Will power. How do you know you had will power? Because you decided against it and never did it again. The problem is that simply labeling the phenomenon "will power" does not explain how you made the decision and were able to stick by it.

Another problem with the will-power concept is the common assumption that strength of will is an inborn characteristic, something like intelligence, that can't be altered significantly by the individual. To the "weak-willed" person, that conclusion means, in effect, that his cause is hopeless. He might as well give up because he was slighted when this magic ingredient was passed out. Actually, if a person doesn't have enough personal power now, it doesn't mean that he never will. It simply means he hasn't developed that level of ability yet. The fact is, we *can* develop the power to effectively direct ourselves.

It is also useful to recognize that personal power is to some extent a "habit-specific" phenomenon. That is, an individual may have an ability to control certain specific behaviors, but he may have difficulty with certain others. I have worked with a number of overweight individuals who defined themselves and were defined by others as being weak willed. But most of these people were highly disciplined in many areas of their lives. Most had learned to control, among other things, their tempers, sexual appetites, and work habits. These individuals were generally on time, responsible, and hard working. In most cases, their personal power problems existed only with respect to their eating behaviors. (In fact, some of these individuals were in such control that compulsive eating was their one tension release.) Understanding this fact is necessary in building faith in self, which is essential to successful self-direction.

We Can Develop Personal Power

To summarize, we may not be able to clearly understand the dynamics of personal power, but it helps to think of it as a skill rather than as an inborn trait. It is also important to recognize that even "out-of-control" people (like overweight individuals) retain their agency and are exercising power over their behavior in many respects. Furthermore, you can improve your personal power even if your understanding of the concept itself is vague. You may not understand the laws of physics and physiology affecting your body as you learn to play tennis, but practice, feedback, and persistence will still improve your ability. Personal power is no different. With practice, feedback, and persistence, you can increase your power.

Chapter 3

Faith Is the Basis of Personal Power

If you want access to the ultimate power in the universe, look to God. Faith (meaning a knowledge that God exists *and* an assurance that your behavior conforms to his wishes) allows you to tie into the power by which worlds are formed and governed. Obviously, this is the ultimate personal power available, and more will be said about it in the next chapter.

For now, we need to consider a more basic issue. How do we develop the self-direction ability necessary to put our lives in conformity with Christ's teachings? If we are to do so, faith in ourselves—or self-confidence—is one of the most important requirements. In fact, faith is the key to motivation in general. A person moves toward a goal if (1) he has faith that the outcome will be worth the effort, and (2) he believes in his ability to accomplish the goal. To grow personally, we therefore need to have faith in correct principles *and* faith in our ability to live them.

An individual may believe that church activity is important, yet he may stay away from church. The barrier to success in such a case is not a lack of desire to achieve, but a lack of faith in the personal possibility of achieving. The person may think, "I can't live by those standards. They won't accept me. I'll look like a fool." Those with little self-confidence are often caught between wanting to accomplish some worthwhile goal and feeling unable to do so.

A lack of faith in himself also leads a person to make either very high-risk or very low-risk decisions. When you make a low-risk decision, you usually decide not to do something at all. (Sam had this problem in an earlier example.) Deciding not to go to school, not to study, not to be active in the Church, not to accept a social invitation, not to ask a question, not to ask for a raise, or not to do a multitude of similar things becomes a way of life for the individual lacking faith in himself. He accomplishes very little because he seldom tries anything important. (Important things usually involve the risk of failure.) He is often a passive rather than an active participant in life, a reactor rather than an actor.

High-risk decisions, on the other hand, involve goals in which the chances of success are remote. People often select high-risk goals because such goals make rationalization possible. If a person is successful with a high-risk goal, it can be very satisfying, especially because of the low odds of success. But if he fails, which is much more likely, the individual can be philosophical about it. "Oh, well, what can I expect?" Failure can then be blamed on the difficult nature of the goal, or on a lack of committed effort, rather than on a lack of ability.

Obviously, in order to be successful, a person must generally make decisions involving moderate risk. Too many low-risk choices leave us short of our potential, while a preponderance of high-risk goals can lead to excessive failure. Unfortunately, the lower a person's self-esteem, the likelier he is to make either low-risk or very high-risk decisions. For example, someone wanting to lose weight but having little faith in his ability to do so may decide not to diet at all—a low-risk choice. Or he may set an overly simplistic goal, such as reading several books on dieting, which is certainly a first step but will not solve the weight problem without application—another low-risk choice. Conversely, he might adopt high-risk goals, such as doing away with all sweets forever, or engaging in strenuous exercise for one hour every day. He is not likely to sustain either of these high-risk choices for long. More moderate-risk goals for weight loss, such as cutting back on snacking and increasing his level of exercise gradually, would be more appropriate.

Faith in self is critical in both the selection and attainment of goals. It is also a basic factor in personal motivation. Therefore, building faith in ourselves is one of the most important things we can do in developing personal power. Following are some suggestions on how we can strengthen ourselves in this respect.

Personal Testimony Tactics

One method of building or strengthening faith in ourselves is to become converted to a sense of our inherent worth and value. Many people *believe* that they have eternal value, but they are not necessarily *converted* to the fact. Others believe in the infinite worth of human beings in general, but forget that they themselves fall into that category.

We can be converted to a sense of our worth in much the same way as we develop our faith in the gospel. A person investigating the restored Church needs to study Church doctrine and to think deeply about its implications. He must also pray in order to obtain a spiritual confirmation. His third step is to apply teachings of the Church and to note the personal benefit of living by gospel principles. These three steps—study, prayer, and work—also apply to becoming *converted* to a sense of one's own worth and value.

First, think about your worth. Moses did, and he made the following observations:

> And it came to pass that Moses looked upon Satan and said: Who art thou? For behold, I am a son of God, in the similitude of his Only Begotten; and where is thy glory, that I should worship thee?

Get thee hence, Satan; deceive me not; for God said unto me: Thou art after the similitude of mine Only Begotten. (Moses 1:13, 16.)

As with Moses, so with us. How can we possibly be close to the Lord and his teachings without understanding how important we are? Why was this world created? To give *us* experience. Why did God give his Only Begotten Son? For *us*. What is the purpose of the gospel? To give *us* eternal opportunity. Whose children are *we*? God's. What is *our* potential? To become like him. The conclusion seems inescapable: We (including *you*) must be terribly important in the eternal scheme of things.

A second step in becoming converted to an idea of your worth is to pray about it. When is the last time you thought to pray for a conviction of *your* importance to the Lord? Not many do. People often pray for help with negative feelings, or for help in controlling undesired behavior and circumstances, but few pray for an understanding or conviction of their eternal value. Do it occasionally. You need more than an intellectual conviction of your worth; you need a spiritual assurance.

The third step is to act on the assumption of worth. Even though negative feelings and fear remain, assume that you are a person of worth and act as if you were. This means going to social gatherings and acting as if you were equal in value to others in the group, even if you feel inferior. It means praying as if you were loved by the Lord even if you feel unloved. It means attempting projects even when you feel incompetent. You may feel strange doing this at first, but only because of a misguided feeling about your self-worth. The fact is that everyone does have inherent value, and thus each is justified in feeling good about himself.

Other helpful practices in building faith in yourself are described below. Keep in mind that you need to repeat these faith-building steps over time. Many are converted to the gospel but then fail to continue to study, pray, and work. Testimony, of course, dies if left unattended. Faith in ourselves is no different. We need to keep nurturing it.

Be Charitable With Yourself

A large percentage of the people I deal with professionally have lived or are living in an environment in which they feel that they are constantly being criticized by those close to them. What they do never seems good enough. "Thanks for taking out the garbage, *but* you left those papers over there." "Why can't you . . . ?" "Why don't you ever . . . ?" "I can't trust you." "You're capable of so much more."

Assume that you are in that situation, and that someone close to you (husband, wife, parents, roommate) is constantly negative, and rarely supportive of the things you do. You will find that your self-confidence is sooner or later affected by the criticism. We don't normally do well when we are consistently put down—yet many make a habit of regularly criticizing themselves. Obviously, the impact on a person is no less harmful—indeed, probably more harmful—when the lack of acceptance comes from himself rather than another.

It's interesting that some of those who are critical of themselves are also very concerned about being charitable with others. Ironically, they may even put themselves down for being negative with someone else. ("You dummy, why are you so critical?") They understand that criticism is hurtful to others, but they overlook the fact that it also hurts when directed inward. It should also be noted that, in spite of their good intentions, those who are critical of themselves are almost always critical of others.

Monitor over several days the number of times you say or think critical things about yourself. Many who have tried this are astounded at how regularly they put themselves down. For many, in fact, self-criticism has become such a habit that it occurs without their awareness. They come to self-condemning conclusions automatically, without being aware of the thought processes involved. They then end up feeling bad about themselves "for no good reason."

Simply being aware of self-critical thought will usually tend to minimize it. Where negative thought continues, it is useful to say "stop" to yourself immediately on becoming aware of a self-critical comment, and then to replace the negative thought with a more productive one. This simple procedure, if consistently applied, will normally solve the problem.

Minimize self-criticism, and your faith in yourself will increase. Increased faith in self, in turn, increases personal power.

Want Positive Results? Think Positive Thoughts

Along with limiting self-criticism, another helpful practice is to recognize your accomplishments and to think positive thoughts about yourself. You need to appreciate the good things you do and privately compliment yourself, even for relatively routine achievements. Some people compliment themselves only for out-of-the-ordinary, very unusual accomplishments. Unfortunately, using that standard, it's usually a long stretch between compliments. People need to feed their self-confidence more regularly.

If you don't feel that you do anything noteworthy, remember that sometimes it's a significant achievement just to get out of bed in the morning. Millions seem almost permanently attached to the mattress some days. You may not get promoted tomorrow, but you can still recognize and appreciate the tasks you complete at work. You may not deserve Mother-of-the-Year recognition on any given day, but you can still appreciate the little things you do on behalf of your family (even if they don't seem to). By appreciating little things, you build your personal power to accomplish greater things.

In talking with Richard, it became apparent to me that he seldom complimented himself. In fact, he was convinced that he was a failure and that he rarely did anything of worth. However, during one brief conversation, the following came to light. Richard is:

—a high priest
—faithful in Church assignments
—honest with others

—true to his wife
—a manager in a respected firm
—sensitive to others
—rarely late
—prompt in paying bills
—respectful of his body
—consistent in doing what is asked of him
—a nurturing father
—able to keep confidences
—unselfish
—hard working
—relatively intelligent
—dedicated to principles

These attributes and virtues just scratch the surface of what could be said. Many instances, unnoticed by Richard, demonstrated his accomplishments and worth—even on this particular day when he was feeling so negative about himself.

Actually, Richard is like many others in that he is afraid to compliment himself out of fear that doing so leads to pride, or inhibits motivation to do good works. On the contrary—when we have faith in ourselves, our *desire* to do the right thing increases, along with our *ability* to live correctly. Those who are convinced of their worth and potential do not ignore faults in their behavior, but are actually better able to recognize them. On the other hand, those lacking self-confidence are often incapable or afraid of recognizing their limitations, and thus cover up their perceived inadequacies by acting conceited, stubborn, unwilling to learn, and, in a word, proud.

You Might Not Be So Bad After All

Perfectionistic thinking, or unrealistic expectation, is a common cause of low personal power. It is surprising to see the number of successful people who feel that they are failures. These individuals are often highly respected people, but they feel inferior because they fall short of their own standards. In their minds, they must be *the* best, or close to it, in every respect before they can accept themselves. Perfection, as these individuals have defined it, is usually not attainable in the mortal sphere; thus, as long as they maintain unrealistic expectations, these people are doomed by their own definition to perpetual feelings of low self-esteem.

Because of our high standards, the tendency to become anxious about our self-improvement goals may be more prevalent among Latter-day Saints than others. Our standards are certainly above those of the world, and often above the standards of other religious denominations. Latter-day Saints are aiming at more than simply avoiding behaviors that hurt others. Our goal is complete self-mastery, in preparation for sharing in all of the power and glory of this world's creator. An exciting thought—but also a depressing one unless we remember that complete self-mastery is a one-step-at-a-time proposition. Many look at where they are and at where they want to be, and then get depressed at the distance they have yet to travel. Some get so discouraged that they forsake their goals altogether.

This sometimes happens because of a tendency I like to call "Sundayitis." This is our unfortunate tendency to evaluate our performance against that of others. In so doing we almost always compare others at their best (as they appear on Sunday) with us at our worst. Brother and Sister Johnson and their children look nearly perfect sitting on the bench in sacrament meeting. What isn't obvious is how Sister Johnson sometimes yells at her kids, has a messy house at times (never when you have seen it), and has serious emotional disturbances that she keeps hidden from public view.

The fact is that none of us is perfect, and we are all in this thing together. A more detailed discussion of this issue can be found in *The Art of Effective Living* referred to earlier. There it is pointed out that some conclude that they are two or three laps behind everybody else in life's race, and that therefore they have to run twice as hard and make only half as many errors as everyone else in order to catch up. Having unrealistic expectations and trying too hard will lower personal power and may lead to a problem similar to the one illustrated some years ago by Harry Emerson Fosdick:

> One boy had shone in the limited community where he was born. He was the pride of his large family and alike the handsomest and ablest boy in the town. In everything he undertook he was always first, and he grew into young manhood a serious, high-minded youth, headed for one of the major professions but with a dangerous factor in his situation of which he was unaware—a dominant picture of his desired self as always in shining first. Then in a large university he found himself good but not eminent. The expectations of peerless priority, built into him by his family and friends, proved fallacious. He suffered a serious nervous breakdown without knowing why. Only when he found out why, saw clearly the absurd tension between his actual and imagined self, and went through a thorough process of self-acceptance did he get himself in hand and go on to make a creditable and serviceable use of the self he really had. (*On Being a Real Person*, Harper and Brothers, 1943, p. 55.)

Again, whenever we expect too much or too little of ourselves, we are likely to fall short of our best possible performance. The feeling of forever falling short reduces our self-confidence and undermines our personal power. If you seldom feel successful, chances are that your goals or expectations are too high.

Good People Do Bad Things (Occasionally)

Some people have a hard time accepting themselves because they do, or have done, unacceptable things. In order to accept ourselves even though we are not perfect, we should understand that behavior and thoughts are not fundamental parts of us. Yes, we are responsible for what we think and do, but we also have power to change both our behavior and our attitudes. As a matter of fact, behavior and attitudes change continually. But there is something about you and me—spirit, intelligence, soul— that is fundamental and does not necessarily change with changes in behavior and attitudes. We can at least accept that fundamental part of us that we call spirit, even if we cannot accept totally our thoughts and behavior at any given moment.

To draw an analogy, the impact of food on our bodies is similar to the impact of behavior and attitudes in defining our worth. What I had for breakfast this morning is now a part of me, in a sense, but in a larger sense I am something much more than that. If what I ate was unpleasant or unhealthy, I can avoid it in the future. The fact that I ate something bad does not mean that I am bad. But then, if I were to continue eating incorrectly over time, my whole body would begin to suffer.

Likewise, if a person's behavior and attitudes are negative, they eventually affect fundamental spirit and intelligence. But still there is something about you and me that is much more important than our attitudes and behavior at any given point in time. If I think or do something bad, it does not mean that I am bad. It helps to remember this fact and not to judge yourself too harshly or prematurely just because you are not yet perfect.

To further illustrate that you and I have value and worth independent of what we do, think of the brain-damaged individual paralyzed from birth and, therefore, unable to do productive, positive things—never able to serve others, never able to take care of himself. Does he lack value? Shouldn't we discard such a person? No right-thinking person would eliminate that life for *any* amount of money. A living, breathing child of God has infinite value under any circumstance. As living, breathing children of God, so do you and I.

A final thought on this subject: The next time you do something silly, remember that smart people do stupid things. Members of my family are relatively bright people, yet they (including me) have done some of the most stupid things—like throwing an anchor into the water without a rope attached; trying to drive the truck with camper into the garage, which has an eight-foot clearance; locking keys in the car twice in the same month; and dropping a boat off its trailer a good fifty feet away from the water. Oh, well! Smart people do dumb things!

Set Moderate-Risk Goals

Effective goals have the advantage of giving us both direction and motivation. Ineffective goals give us neither. As indicated earlier, goals that are set too low leave us short of our potential. Goals that are too high contribute to excessive failure and misdirected effort. Relating these outcomes to self-confidence, if we seldom achieve meaningful goals in our life, we lose important opportunities to feel good about ourselves. If we are seldom successful, we have all too many opportunities to feel like failures.

Since everyone's level of personal power is different, an appropriate goal for one person is likely to be too high or too low for another. Goals must be personalized. For example, Mark wants to be more socially outgoing. At present, he seldom reaches out to people and he has few friends. Mark shouldn't expect to completely change his approach to others overnight, but he could set a goal to say "hello" to one or two new people a day. He could set a goal to smile more, and he might sign himself up for a class or some activity involving social opportunity. Mark needs to push himself, but not too far, too fast.

As you select personal goals, go primarily for those involving a moderate risk of failure. That is, choose a goal that will take effort on your part, but that is clearly within reach. By doing this you maximize your chance of meaningful success, which then builds faith and personal power.

Trying Too Hard Will Get You in Trouble

Remember, making a measured effort—as opposed to trying too hard—is an important consideration in building faith in yourself. Yet, people commonly assume that someone who is unsuccessful with a self-improvement goal is not trying hard enough. They often conclude that if someone wants something badly enough, or if he is really committed, he *will* do it. On the contrary, the problem is often too much rather than too little motivation.

Stan, for example, was trying to control his temper. Unfortunately, he often got so intensely involved in trying to reach his goal that the problem was almost always on his mind. Stan thought constantly about his unruly temper and about its negative impact on his family. In the process, he became self-critical and oversensitive to comments from the family, which reduced his personal power.

Thinking about the problem continually also led Stan to remember factors related to his anger. Each time he lost his temper, Stan analyzed the situation at length, trying to figure out where he went wrong. Doing so led him to focus again on the events to which he had reacted angrily in the first place. He was trying to solve his problem through self-examination, but by thinking about the situation anew, he found himself getting upset all over again. Thoughts like, "She had no right to do that," and, "I won't stand to be treated like that," led to more anger. And, of course, the increase in anger contradicted his goal.

By being overconcerned, Stan also overreacted in general to situations. Everyone develops feelings of anger at times in family relationships. But as Stan felt himself getting emotional in certain situations, he panicked out of fear that he would lose control again. This panic usually created a surge of emotion that clouded his reasoning and further weakened his personal power. Ironically, Stan's fear of losing control (resulting from virtually constant thought about the problem) increased the probability of his losing control.

A person like Stan, who is committed to a difficult self-improvement goal, may be tempted to try harder. Remember, however, that being overconcerned about self-improvement is sometimes one of the biggest obstacles to successful goal attainment. In fact, extremes are usually counterproductive no matter what the issue, and that is certainly the case with respect to self-improvement. It is possible to not care enough. Nephi describes those who take life too lightly, saying that they will be disappointed eventually as a result (2 Nephi 28:7-8). For others, however, the problem is one of being overly concerned about improving. In Stan's case, overconcern created more problems than it solved.

Another problem with trying too hard is that we can get so busy putting pressure on ourselves that we are not able to attend to the factors that make self-direction possible. For several years, Renee tried desperately to control her weight. Whenever she would overeat or have something that was on her forbidden list (which happened as often as not), Renee became severely self-critical. "You dummy! You fat slob! You keep blowing it time after time!" Renee got so involved in this almost ritualized self-hate program that she never thought to ask questions, such as: "What factors were associated with my decision to eat that bag of potato chips? What activity was I engaged in at the time? How could I avoid that behavior in the future? Are my goals reasonable? How can I build faith in myself?" In other words, Renee was engaged in punishing herself for the act, rather than in planning how to overcome the problem. Having been severely punished, it was almost as if she had atoned for the sin and was free to eat again.

Renee also became more convinced with each failure and with each bout of self-punishment that she was indeed a weak-willed, no-good person, virtually incapable of controlling herself. Since she had earlier learned to eat in response to frustration and depression, her negative thoughts about herself ("You dummy!") actually increased her "need" to eat. She soon began to feel that she would never solve her eating problems. She then concluded that she might as well eat and enjoy it since she couldn't help herself anyway. With that conclusion, all power to control her eating behavior was lost.

Let's Build Faith in Ourselves

This chapter has emphasized the fact that we don't develop personal power without first having faith in ourselves. Of course, as we develop personal power, faith grows. This cyclical pattern (faith in self leads to personal power, which leads to more faith in self, which leads to more personal power) repeats itself over and over as we grow and progress. Unfortunately, it also works the other way. As we lose faith in ourselves, personal power is lost, which further reduces our faith in ourselves, and so on.

Look back over the section headings in this chapter. Each one indicates an important factor in building faith in your ability to take charge of your life. Other ideas with respect to this most important issue are presented in subsequent chapters.

Chapter 4

The Spiritual Element in Personal Power

The techniques and suggestions offered elsewhere in this book are compatible with the teachings of the Savior, but they do not emphasize the special strength available to the individual who is committed to the gospel. Putting ourselves on the Lord's side requires self-direction, but it also makes developing personal power easier in many ways. This chapter will discuss the nature of the spiritual help available and how to use it.

The Lord Can Be There When We Have Power Failures

The Apostle Paul made an observation several different times in his writings: "There hath no temptation taken you but such as is common to man: but God is faithful, who will not suffer you to be tempted above that ye are able; but will with the temptation also make a way to escape, that ye may be able to bear it" (1 Corinthians 10:13).

Here Paul indicates that a way is always provided whereby we might escape evil. Apparently, no one can correctly say that his lack of personal power is due to overpowering circumstances in his life. Paul's statement also suggests the possibility of the Lord's active involvement in helping us avoid temptation.

Linda was aware of Paul's statement and similar scriptures, but she seriously questioned their relevance in her case. Linda had experienced some very serious complications in her life. Her second marriage had just ended due to her husband's infidelity. Both her first and second spouses had left home for other women, leaving Linda with two small children and considerable debt. Linda obtained a good job but soon lost it, primarily because of a chronic health problem that had flared up just after she took the position. To cap it off, on the day I first talked with her, Linda's car had just broken down and she had no way to look for work.

Linda was convinced that she was being tested beyond her limit. "I try so hard to do the right thing and it seems like nothing helps," she said. "I have prayed long and hard for help, but nothing seems to happen except more problems." Linda was depressed, discouraged, and running low on faith.

Linda probably was at the limit of her endurance. Interestingly, her life began to fall into place from the point described here. As she thought about it, she realized that circumstances in her life had lightened and events had turned more positive just after each particularly low point. There were many times, however, during periods of depression, when she lost faith temporarily, and assumed that she had been abandoned by the Lord. When she came to this conclusion, it was usually due to one or more of the misunderstandings suggested below.

Why We Sometimes Feel Abandoned by the Lord

We sometimes feel abandoned by the Lord because, in a sense, we are. The Lord allows us to solve some problems on our own, even in situations in which we doubt our ability. Linda in the example above assumed that she could not cope when, in fact, she could. Life gives us the opportunity to learn about our capabilities under pressure. The Lord knows what we're capable of, but we don't always have this knowledge. Sometimes we think, "I couldn't handle that. I would never be able to stand a problem like that," only to find that when the test comes, we too are capable beyond our expectations. Some, of course, give up prematurely and give in to alcohol, drugs, immorality, and suicide. But the individual with faith in himself and in divine power need not do so. He can rest assured that temptation and trials are not beyond his ability to handle them. Circumstances will change if and when the breaking point is reached.

In addition to selling herself short, Linda's requests of her Eternal Father were sometimes ineffective or misdirected. Oliver Cowdery, in sections 8 and 9 of the Doctrine and Covenants, was given some useful suggestions regarding how to seek the Lord. Among other instructions, he was told: "Remember that without faith you can do nothing; therefore ask in faith. Trifle not with these things; do not ask for that which you ought not" (D&C 8:10).

Linda sometimes made her requests without really expecting that they would be honored. She asked, but not in faith. At other times, she asked for that which she "ought not." Linda spent considerable energy praying that her husband would return to her. This request was inappropriate for at least two reasons. In the first place, Linda probably would have been worse off had her husband returned. She assumed that getting her husband back was the solution to all of her problems, but the Lord knew better. Secondly, the Lord would have had to violate her husband's agency in order to grant her request— something he simply will not do. A prayer that her husband's heart might be touched would have been appropriate; but, of course, many people whose hearts are touched remain unmoved anyway. Free agency is a fundamental principle and cannot be violated.

Linda also had a tendency to put issues before the Lord without first of all doing what she could to solve them herself. In section 9 of the Doctrine and Covenants, Oliver Cowdery was told: "Behold, you have not understood; you have supposed that I would give it unto you, when you took no thought save it was to ask me" (D&C 9:7).

In Linda's case, she often prayed for help that she might feel better, or that she might not be so depressed. But unfortunately, she often made little or no effort to change the negative thinking that created her feelings. Nor did she force herself to be active in ways that would help her feel better. Rather, she often made the choice to sit and "think" (sulk).

True, during her depressed periods, the Lord might inspire someone to call or he might create some other event to occur (which happened when she both needed it *and* when she had done all she could to help herself). Also, the Spirit might give Linda constructive ideas on how to solve her problem. For instance, she might be inspired to call someone, to read a particular book, or to engage in some activity. But again, Linda always has the choice of whether to follow such suggestions or not, and this kind of assistance usually waits on her efforts to help herself. The wise parent helps with homework but doesn't do it *for* the child. We have divine help available to us, but it comes after, or in conjunction with, our best efforts.

Look for Divine Help in Several Ways

We are not always helped in the ways we expect, or as quickly as we hope—but we are helped when assistance is needed, and when it fits in with our life's plan. Some of the ways in which the Lord will intervene are suggested below.

The Circumstances We Face May Be Changed

The fact that faith can remove sickness and prevent accidents is well documented and often experienced by Latter-day Saints. Most of the world's inhabitants at present have medical technology available to prevent and overcome sickness. Latter-day Saints also have faith and priesthood at their disposal. Many people have avoided the debilitating consequences of illness in their lives or have been spared the trauma of serious accidents through the intervention of this power.

Of course, the Lord has absolute control over all this world's events. Normally, those events operate independently of his direct intervention (for good or bad) in order to comprise the curriculum of life for us all. However, when we have both faith and need, events and circumstances can be altered. Many people have been blessed by amazing sets of circumstances that definitely have the mark of divine engineering.

Our Thoughts Can Be Influenced

If we have faith, we can expect warnings regarding moral or emotional danger. We can be directly warned by the Spirit against entering relationships or participating in activities that threaten our personal power. Listening may be difficult, but if we ask appropriately and in faith, the warning and direction will be there.

The Lord can, and will, under the right conditions, help us get educated, find employment, and make appropriate financial decisions. We can receive information regarding whom to marry, how to raise our children, and how to make relationships work smoothly. Good ideas, constructive information, and how-to instruction are all available.

Home computers are becoming very popular. One of their advantages is their capability of tapping into information systems of astounding breadth. When we are in top spiritual form, we have access to something infinitely better—the Master File for the universe! We can receive direct revelation from the fountain of all truth regarding any number of personal needs. Certainly there are limits on what any given mortal can understand and utilize from the Master File, but what we need to know for our own personal needs can be made available to us.

Emotion and motivation are controlled by our thoughts—our attitudes, assumptions, and conclusions about ourselves and the world. This means that if we effectively seek for the guidance of the Spirit, we can have direct help with our *feelings* as well as with our understanding.

With respect to the impact of the Spirit on both feelings and understanding, the Lord told Hyrum Smith through his brother Joseph: "Verily, verily, I say unto you, I will impart unto you of my Spirit, which shall enlighten your mind, which shall fill your soul with joy; And then shall ye know, or by this shall you know, all things whatsoever you desire of me, which are pertaining unto things of righteousness, in faith believing in me that you shall receive" (D&C 11:13-14).

The Spirit can enlighten both our feelings (help us feel joy) and our intellect. But, of course, in addition to divine influence on our thinking, the negative influence of Lucifer and those who work with him is also with us. Still other negative or counter-productive ideas are self-generated, based on our experiences. In the final analysis, we must choose our own attitudes and reach our own conclusions. No power, divine or satanic, will rob us of that opportunity and responsibility. But if we choose to heed the divine promptings, we can expect to be inspired with good ideas that will help us to make productive decisions and to have good feelings.

The Lord May Help Others Help Us·

Parents, a bishop, a friend, a counselor, a doctor, all may be given ideas or instruction by the Spirit that will help us. Sometimes the help for us comes through someone else because of his faith; at other times, our faith is responsible. The result, obviously, is the same either way. We can be instructed, befriended, motivated, or otherwise helped through the agency of others. Many examples exist of someone calling at just the right moment to make a difference in a person's life, money received when needed most, life-altering advice in a letter or personal communication, and so forth.

However, it should be pointed out that help from others may at times be hard to recognize. Certainly, being helped by another requires humility and receptivity on our part under any circumstance, but sometimes what we get may seem more harmful than helpful. This may be because the help we need at that precise moment is a test of our faith, a rebuke, an opportunity to forgive someone who has offended us, or a chance to learn to love an enemy. Whatever help is needed, the bottom line is that if we are faithful, we can rest assured that we will receive the assistance we need to reach our righteous goals.

The Lord Can Reinforce Us

Chapter 7 discusses setting up situations in which we reinforce ourselves in the short run as we work toward goals that have payoffs primarily in the long term. The Spirit can also work with us in this regard. For example, we can receive direct information from the Spirit regarding whether we are right or wrong. (See 1 John 4:6; 1 Nephi 22:2; Jacob 4:13; D&C 11:12, 76:10, and 130:9, among many other scriptures.)

Immediate and consistent reward for desired behavior, and punishment for undesired behavior, can be helpful in building personal power. To the person open to this kind of help, it is one of the things the Spirit can provide. You can have an immediate recognition of appropriate behavior (and corresponding good feelings), as well as an immediate recognition of doing wrong.

Burdens and Cares Can Be Lifted

Self-direction, especially emotional self-direction, can be easier for the person committed to the gospel. On one hand, the individual can be forgiven for his trespasses. Many have experienced the profound relief that comes from repentance and forgiveness. If you have not had this experience personally, read the account of Alma (Alma 36:12-20) to understand the emotional impact of being blessed with forgiveness. Developing personal power is possible only if you are free of the weight of guilt on your shoulders.

Faith can also help you avoid worrying about troublesome events in your life. In 1 Peter 5:6-7, a group of early Saints were instructed, "Humble yourselves therefore under the mighty hand of God, that he may exalt you in due time: Casting all your care upon him; for he careth for you." If we have faith in God, we also have faith that all things will work for our good (D&C 100:15). We have faith that righteousness will triumph (D&C

3:16; 65:2). We know that "His purposes fail not, neither are there any who can stay his hand" (D&C 76:3). That assurance can create calm when evil seems to triumph and when events appear overwhelming. Of all the things you may worry about—including world conditions, personal finances, health, relationships, personal and family security—most become relatively unimportant when you really believe that all things will work to your advantage as you keep the faith.

Another advantage of faith is the relief that it can afford from hateful feelings. Paul counseled in Romans 12:19, "Dearly beloved, avenge not yourselves, but rather give place unto wrath: for it is written, Vengeance is mine; I will repay, saith the Lord." Many people who have been offended essentially ruin their lives by letting hate or anger develop to the point that it disturbs their emotional peace. They may also stop going to church, pull away from relationships, or violate law and common sense in an effort to get even. All of this can be avoided by the individual who leaves the matter to the Lord and who can rest assured that justice (or mercy) will eventually triumph.

Faith Can Give Us Power Over Satan

Naturally, Satan will attempt to thwart our efforts to discipline and improve ourselves. Happily, faith in God is an effective weapon against the adversary. Joseph Smith, at the beginning of this dispensation, was almost overcome by Lucifer as he attempted to make contact with his Creator. In describing this experience, Joseph said:

> But, exerting all my powers to call upon God to deliver me out of the power of this enemy which seized upon me, and at the very moment when I was ready to sink into despair and abandon myself to destruction—not to an imaginary ruin, but to the power of some actual being from the unseen world, who had such marvelous power as I had never before felt in any being—just at this moment of great alarm, I saw a pillar of light exactly over my head, above the brightness of the sun, which descended gradually until it fell upon me.
>
> It no sooner appeared than I found myself delivered from the enemy which held me bound. (Joseph Smith—History 1:16-17.)

Lucifer has significant power, but his power yields to the omnipotence of God. We can call on God's power to protect us from the influence of Satan. The scriptures instruct us to "Pray always, that you may come off conqueror; yea, that you may conquer Satan, and that you may escape the hands of the servants of Satan that do uphold his work" (D&C 10:5).

Becoming a Friend of God

As suggested at the outset of this chapter, divine help can be a great asset in developing personal power. Faith can result in better physical and emotional health, which obviously play an important part in personal power; faith can also result in direct effort by the Lord in helping us reach our righteous goals. We would feel quite pleased and fortunate if the chairman of the board of the corporation we worked for was a close, personal friend, committed to helping us develop our full potential within the corporation. Since the creator of this world has offered to be our friend (D&C 84:77), and since he is committed to helping us develop our full potential (Moses 1:39), it makes good sense to take him up on the offer.

Becoming a friend of God has been the subject of many volumes and countless sermons in each of the gospel dispensations. The steps in the process of becoming a friend of God are familiar to most Latter-day Saints. They include study of the scriptures in order to know God and better understand his thinking; prayer and fasting in order to communicate with him; and committing ourselves to a set of values and behavior consistent with his. The more progress we make in these respects, the stronger our faith and commitment. The stronger our faith and commitment, the more we are able to receive divine intervention and influence in our lives.

Some people get discouraged, however, and don't seek the Lord because, in their minds, they have not adequately prepared themselves. "I am unworthy of the Lord's blessings," they conclude, "therefore, why seek them?" One problem with this conclusion is that it involves a mere mortal making the Lord's decision for him. Some people undoubtedly are unworthy of the Lord's blessings, but the Lord should be the judge of that. Another point to remember is that we don't have to be perfect in order to receive blessings from the Lord. In fact, we need his help to become perfect. Waiting until you have stopped sinning before you pray for help is like waiting until you are at your ideal weight before going on a weight-reduction program. Neither makes much sense.

Again, Brigham Young has given us some practical suggestions regarding seeking the Lord whether we feel worthy or not.

> Have you prayers in your families? "Yes, sometimes, but I do not always feel like praying, and then I feel as though it would be a sin."
>
> Let me tell you how you should do. If you feel that you are tempted not to open your mouth to the Lord, and as though the heavens are brass over your heads and the earth iron beneath your feet, and that everything is closed up, and you feel that it would be a sin for you to pray, then walk up to the devil and say, Mr. Devil, get out of my way; and if you feel that you cannot get down upon your knees, and if they don't feel right when they are down, put something under them, some sharp sticks, for instance, and say, knees come to it. "But I dare not open my mouth," says one, "for fear that I shall swear." Then say, "open mouth, and now tongue, begin. Cannot I say Father? Yes, I can: I learned that in the days of my youth." Suppose you say, "Father, look in mercy upon me," do you think the devil is going to snap you up then? If he is still by, and you dare not open your eyes for fear you will see him, tell him to stand there until you have done praying, and bring the body to a state of submission. (*Journal of Discourses* 3:207.)

We should not avoid requesting the help we need just because we may not feel worthy of receiving it. But it makes exceptionally good sense for us to do everything we can to put ourselves in tune so that there will be no question of our ability to receive strength and assistance from the Lord when it is needed.

The Power of Commitment

We have discussed the fact that the Lord will intervene in our lives as needed to help us reach important goals. There is also a power that we can gain by simply being committed to the gospel. Deep commitment to an ideal can be exceptionally motivating, even when the ideal is not so ideal. For example, several Irish Republican Army terrorists gave their lives as a result of self-imposed fasts in the Maze Prison outside Belfast. Assuming that these terrorists were guilty of murder and of other crimes with which they were charged, it is obvious that their strength didn't come from the Lord. Commitment to a cause, just or unjust, can be highly motivating.

Of course, many others have been martyred or endured great privations for different causes, some as meaningless to the common good as setting a record for rowing across the Pacific or jumping cars with a motorcycle. The point here is that dedication to a cause is inherently motivating. Once we are committed to the gospel, that same drive and intense concern can motivate us in healthy, productive ways. Commitment to the gospel gives us added strength to do those things that bring happiness and joy into our lives.

Being committed also simplifies life. Many questionable choices are eliminated and a great deal of energy can be saved when you have a "rod of iron" (1 Nephi 8:19) to hang onto and to use as a guide. When you are committed to the principles of the gospel, you don't have to wonder whether or not you should live the Word of Wisdom, attend meetings on Sunday, emphasize family over career, avoid close male-female relationships outside of marriage, and so forth. As the Savior said: "Come unto me, all ye that labour and are heavy laden, and I will give you rest. Take my yoke upon you, and learn of me; for I am meek and lowly in heart: and ye shall find rest unto your souls. For my yoke is easy, and my burden is light" (Matthew 11:28-30).

Living can be easier if you are committed to the gospel; for example, you will probably experience fewer worries, less anger, better health, and more structured decisions. However, we cannot ignore the fact that it is sometimes difficult to dedicate ourselves to the gospel. Certainly the converted disciple also has his share of trials and confusion in life—as part of the plan he agreed to. But the fact remains that commitment to the gospel and to the guidelines it provides in decision making can simplify our lives as we grow in faith and dedication.

Another advantage of commitment to the gospel is that it can make temptations easier to deal with. Chapter 5 talks about behavior chains, in which an undesirable behavior is preceded by a whole series of behaviors. For instance, adultery normally doesn't just happen, but begins with interest outside of marriage, time together that results in emotional bonding, relatively minor physical indiscretions such as hugging and kissing and so forth. A person who is dedicated to the gospel will be more likely to recognize inappropriate behaviors earlier in the behavior chain than would those with more worldly values. Since it is much easier to say no to activities that result in emotional bonding than it is to say no to physical involvement after bonding occurs, the converted disciple has an easier job avoiding adultery. In a similar way, it is difficult to become an alcoholic if you never have the first drink. The converted disciple has more rules to live by than does someone without faith, but those very rules protect him from serious difficulties.

It is wise, however, not to become overly confident of our ability to avoid temptation. Some have rationalized relatively minor vices with the thought that they were too righteous to ever succumb to serious temptations: "I go to Church, pray, and read the scriptures. I would never be an alcoholic or an adulterer. I know better." The person who is committed to the gospel has a very real advantage in avoiding temptation, but he is not invincible.

Put on the Armor of God

As we have seen, conversion to the gospel strengthens us in many ways. Our motivation for good works increases, our ability to accomplish self-improvement goals is enhanced, and we have help in avoiding evil. Paul used a metaphor in a discourse to Church members at Ephesus to describe the latter point (Ephe-

sians 6:10-18); this same metaphor was used by a heavenly mes-
senger sent to Joseph Smith (D&C 27:15-18). In it we are
instructed to protect ourselves against evil much as a soldier
would prepare himself for battle. Few people would leave their
vital parts exposed to enemy swords or go into battle without
swords of their own.

Our armor against evil consists of learning truth (through
study of the scriptures), living righteously, understanding the
gospel plan, having faith, being dedicated to correct principles,
relying on the Spirit, and praying consistently. It is virtually
impossible for a person to be overpowered by evil if he is protected in this manner. The problem is that, being mortal, we
often tend to let our guards down and forget to protect ourselves
effectively.

Of course, putting on the whole armor of God requires self-
direction. But at the same time, having the armor on makes self-
direction easier. Think of it as a continuous upward spiral. As we
develop more self-management skill, we receive more spiritual
power, which makes it easier to manage ourselves, which gives us
more power, and so on.

Seeing the great help it can be, we should strive to put the
element of spiritual power at the center of our efforts to develop
personal power.

Chapter 5

The Environmental Element: Personal Power From Outside In

Ultimately, only you and I control how we feel and behave. But we cannot deny the fact that life circumstances can exert a strong influence on moods and behavior. Viktor Frankl tells us that it was possible to find meaning and a measure of happiness even in the hell of a Nazi concentration camp (*Man's Search for Meaning*, Boston: Beacon Press, 1962). Others find happiness in spite of debilitating handicaps or personal tragedy. But it is hard to be yourself, and it is difficult to be happy, when your needs are ignored, or when you face a traumatic life circumstance. Personal power, therefore, depends in part on your creating a positive environment around you.

In fact, environment is sufficiently important that Lucifer felt confident that if he could control external circumstances in the world he could guarantee a mortality without sin. If all good behavior were immediately rewarded and all bad behavior immediately punished, only good behavior would be expected. Of course, a life involving this kind of manipulation and control essentially denies free will and was therefore vetoed by a wise Father. Happiness, joy, growth, and moral independence come only through the judicious exercise of free agency. President Spencer W. Kimball expressed the point as follows:

If pain and sorrow and total punishment immediately followed the doing of evil, no soul would repeat a misdeed. If joy and peace and rewards were instantaneously given the doer of good, there would be no evil, all would do good and not because of the rightness of doing good. There would be no test of strength, no development of character, no growth of powers, no free agency, no Satanic controls. ("Tragedy or Destiny," *Improvement Era*, March 1966, pp. 180, 210.)

Satan's plan was rejected and he lost the war, but he continues to do battle. Part of his current strategy apparently involves creating or emphasizing cues and signals in our environment that influence us in a negative direction. He knows that it is possible for us to lock ourselves into unproductive behavior patterns, and to create personal environments in which it is extremely difficult to grow. He is all too willing to assist us in that process.

Actually, we may play into Lucifer's hand by attempting to handle our problems without changing our environment. Many people stubbornly try to change their behavior without changing circumstances related to the problem. Often they feel that removing the temptation is the coward's way. They assume that the more virtuous approach is to keep the temptation present and successfully avoid it. An example of this might be the overweight person who keeps cookies on hand "for company" but doesn't eat them.

The message of this chapter favors the "cowardly" approach. Successful self-direction effort normally requires that we remove temptation and obstacles from our path. Trying to diet while keeping fattening foods handy is an example of needless risk taking, not virtue.

Habits Are Affected by Environment

Normally, when we do something that we shouldn't, or fail to do something that we should, our actions are preceded by an identifiable series of circumstances. Certain events take place in a logical and relatively predictable sequence leading up to the specific behavior in question.

For example, Phil procrastinates doing his homework. On arriving home from school, he invariably heads for the refrigerator. He then flips on the television in the kitchen (just for a "quick look") while he eats. After being engrossed in the television for a while, he either receives or initiates a call to a friend. That call usually involves an invitation to do something that interrupts study. Saying to himself, "Oh, well, I can get to it later," he goes off to participate in the activity.

On those rare occasions when he has nothing else to do or his homework is too pressing to procrastinate, Phil goes to his room to study. Another relatively predictable pattern then emerges. Phil avoids his desk like the plague. Instead, he gathers his school materials together on the floor and flips on the stereo. He then discusses with himself what needs to be done first and how to approach the assignment. Typically, the job looks hopeless on first glance, so Phil turns over to listen to the music "for a second," in order to get inspiration regarding how to proceed. He usually will then close his eyes in order to maximize the value of his meditation. Upon waking up, he finds that it is time for other activities, or an irresistible offer comes in from a friend.

Phil is influenced by cues in his environment that affect his behavior. There is nothing in his environment that *causes* undesirable behavior, but there are many cues that he has so often associated with negative actions that the influence of these cues is almost overpowering. Examples will be given later regarding how to control or eliminate such cues. For now, imagine how much easier it would be for Phil to get to his studies if the television were disconnected or moved from the kitchen. Phil might also disconnect the telephone during his study period, or force himself to use his desk without the stereo. He could reverse his pattern and eat after studying rather than before. Phil might also decide to begin a homework assignment and develop his plan of approach after starting the work, rather than wait for a plan to develop before he begins. We can think of many useful approaches in changing environmental conditions related to Phil's procrastination, once we understand those conditions.

You can also benefit by understanding environmental factors related to habits that you are either trying to establish or break. You gain personal power by being aware of how your environment influences your behavior, and by changing circumstances in your world so that they are compatible with your goals.

How to Know What Environmental Factors Are Influencing Your Behavior

Armchair analysis is the simplest method of determining what events are related to certain behaviors. You can often get a fairly accurate indication of what triggers particular behaviors by just thinking about past experiences and picturing what happened. In attempting to control a particular habit or behavior, answer the following questions.

When do I do it?
—Time of day
—Particular day of week
—Time of month
Where do I do it?
—Exact location(s)
—Alone or with others
What conditions lead me to think about it?
—People that cause thought about it
—Interactions with others related to thinking about it
—Signs, pictures, symbols in environment
—Emotions or feelings prior to the behavior
What behaviors/events precede it?
—Actions of others
—My own actions
—Occurrences in my environment (clock strikes, alarm rings, recurring sounds, recurring events)

If you are trying to establish a positive habit, similar questions are appropriate:

When am I least likely to do it?
—Time of day
—Day of week
—Time of month
When am I almost certain to do it?
—Time of day
—Day of week
—Time of month
Where am I when I try to do it
—Exact location(s)
—Alone or with others?
Where have I been when I have been successful with it?
—Exact location(s)
—Alone or with others
What do I typically do in lieu of the activity?
—What replacement activity occurs and with whom?
—When is the decision made?
What behaviors/environmental events precede the decision
to put the activity off?
—Actions of others
—Own actions
—Occurrences in the environment

However formulated, the goal is to identify the factors in your
environment that seem to be related to behavior you want to
change.

Paper and Pencil Help

An armchair analysis may be sufficient in uncovering environmental factors related to your behavior, but you may need
to begin an ongoing data-collection effort. Since most people are
not naturally accurate observers, especially of their own behavior,
many can benefit from a more formal approach, such as a
behavior diary.

Although completing them can be a chore, behavior diaries
or daily logs are simple-to-use research instruments. An inven-

tory of eating behavior, similar to the one excerpted below, is an example of a behavior diary that might be useful if your goal is to control your eating habits. The excerpt below is part of a log one person created by simply writing headings on a note pad and then entering the information desired when eating occurred.

Time	What / How Much	Where	Activity
7:10 A.M.	1 toast, butter, jam, medium glass milk	kitchen	reading newspaper
8:30 P.M.	1 medium piece chocolate cake, 2 scoops vanilla ice cream	family room	watching TV

Keeping a complete diary of activities as described above is certainly laborious, but people can normally tolerate it for the week or so it takes to identify patterns. To ease the chore a bit, you can record the information some time after the behavior has occurred. (Even good friends might not understand if you whip out a daily log for recordings during a social or business lunch.) You should also understand that the very act of recording behavior is likely to affect the behavior in question. If your goal is to learn about normal patterns, you should attempt to follow your regular routine to the extent possible while completing the behavior log.

Once collected, information about habits can then be analyzed in terms of activities and environmental circumstances related to the undesirable behavior. Even the very limited data excerpted above about an individual's eating habits are sufficient to indicate that, for this person, eating occurs in conjunction with unrelated activities such as reading the newspaper or watching television. He is more likely to successfully change his eating habits if he isolates eating from other activities. He might try limiting his at-home eating to the kitchen table, and he might refrain from watching television, reading the newspaper, or engaging in similar activities while eating.

Daily Logs Can Increase Efficiency

The approach described above is also helpful when you are trying to become more efficient on a daily basis. Helen seemed to be always busy, but she didn't accomplish a lot. Part of the problem involved her daily routine, which became apparent after she recorded her activities over a two-week period, as excerpted below.

Tuesday A.M.

Time	Activity
6:00 - 6:40	Slept in
6:40 - 7:00	Got kids up / room clean-up
7:00 - 7:40	Breakfast / lunch prep and clean-up
7:40 - 8:30	Television / news program
8:30 - 8:50	Received phone call to help with project
8:50 - 9:30	Made phone calls re: project
9:30 - 11:30	Worked at Ted's school
11:30 - 12:00	Television (serial)

Helen made the above recordings at noon. She then did the same thing in the evening for her afternoon schedule, and she recorded her evening activities just before retiring. After-the-fact recordings missed some information, and the times devoted to particular activities were not exactly recorded; however, the information collected was sufficiently accurate and detailed to indicate several problems in Helen's routine.

For example, over the two-week period, Helen was embarrassed to see on paper how frequently she slept in. She also noticed a multitude of television interruptions. Her habit was to have the television on while she worked on various projects. Unfortunately, the programming tended to draw her away from the project at hand for "a few minutes," which often turned into a much longer time. Frequent telephone calls were also determined to be a definite problem, along with several similar recurring complications in her daily schedule.

Helen vaguely understood most of the problems in her schedule prior to her personal research, but there were some surprises. Even where she was not surprised, something magical about recording her activities and seeing the problems in black and white helped Helen come to grips with them.

To solve the problems she had identified, Helen switched from television to radio as background for her home projects, and she set aside blocks of time during which she did not answer the telephone. Helen reasoned that truly important calls would come through later, and that being immediately available to people at all times was simply not necessary. She also found that going to bed earlier, setting aside time for herself early in the morning (as incentive to get up), and drinking a glass of orange juice immediately on arising helped solve her sleep-in problem.

Gathering detailed information about her activities served a dual purpose for Helen. On one hand, it helped her clarify and define some of the problems her environment presented. On the other hand, her research also provided clues as to how to work around or modify those circumstances. Patterns began to emerge that led to ideas about possible solutions. These solutions were then implemented and their impact monitored. Where solutions were ineffective, others were tried, with the end result being a significant increase in efficiency.

What worked for Helen may help you. If you are concerned about your efficiency level, or some similar problem, give it a try. Information about factors related to your behavior can help you increase personal power.

Define the Objective Correctly

Objectives need to be clearly defined in order to maximize self-development success. Unfortunately, objectives are not as easy to define as you might think. One reason for this is that we tend to define our goals only in terms of the specific behavior we are trying to eliminate—the problem is that I have a temper, I procrastinate, I lie, and so on. Or we may define the objective to be something we need to do better: I need to do more genealogical research and temple work, I need to be a better missionary, and so forth. Usually, however, root issues exist that go deeper than the surface problem.

For example, Joan often fudges on the truth, but that isn't her basic problem. Why does she lie? Because she is afraid others will think less of her if she tells the truth. Why is she so concerned about others' opinions? Because she doesn't think much of herself. Why doesn't she think very much of herself? Because she has unrealistic expectations, which means that she is always failing, by her definition. She is also extremely self-critical when she "fails." Obviously, answers for another individual might be different, but for Joan, directing effort at the base issues of perfectionistic thinking and self-criticism will be as important as focusing effort directly on becoming more honest (the surface issue). Lying is a symptom of a deeper problem for Joan, not the main problem itself.

You can usually identify root problems by asking a series of "why" questions, as illustrated in Joan's case. Doing so is important, since self-development effort may otherwise be misdirected. In fact, certain approaches to solving a surface problem can actually aggravate base issues. In Joan's example, great concern about her problem and self-criticism when she was dishonest would decrease self-esteem and therefore increase the probability of her lying.

You Can Work on Both Surface and Root Objectives Simultaneously

Of course, we can work directly on surface issues (unwanted behaviors) at the same time as we are finding solutions to the basic root problems involved. When working on surface issues directly, we should remember that behaviors tend to be linked together (behavior chains). For example, in an earlier example Phil's tendency to put off homework came at the end of a series of behaviors that tended to build on one another. If we label his surface problem as "procrastinating homework," we shift the emphasis to the end of the series of behaviors—in this case, the choice Phil made not to do his work. But it is usually much easier to change behaviors earlier in the chain. For example, Phil had more luck when he defined the surface problem to be turning the television on when he first came home. That was easier to fix than the general procrastination problem, and by eliminating such problems early in the behavior chain, he was able to overcome the general difficulty.

Phil was able to solve his problem by effectively dealing with the surface issue. But overcoming poor study habits or other problems often requires identifying root causes as well. For example, Phil might resent the pressure to study exerted by his parents; he might have a fear of failure associated with schoolwork; or some other basic difficulty might be inhibiting his motivation. If this is the case, a solution needs to be found for the base problem as well as for the surface issue. In any event, the unwanted behavior itself (again, usually a symptom of a more basic problem) can best be modified if you work at points early in the chain of actions leading to that unwanted behavior.

Attacking the problem early in a behavior chain is especially important when sexual behavior is the issue. Intensity of arousal, of course, builds with time, and is much more difficult to turn off at higher levels. Rather than petting, the problem may be better defined as the habit of a young couple spending too much time alone together, particularly late at night. In a similar vein, the problem may not be immoral conduct so much as it is the habit of dwelling on sexual thoughts, or the problem of putting oneself in a location where sexual stimuli are pronounced. An unacceptable end behavior is always preceded by other behaviors (thoughts are considered here to be "behavior"). You can obtain greater success by defining the real problems as those events that occur early in the behavior sequence.

We usually avoid stressing factors early in behavior chains because these activities seem so harmless. A couple's moral values may allow them to spend considerable amounts of time kissing without feeling guilty. They therefore are reluctant to define extended kissing as *the* problem. But in order to maximize one's success in avoiding premarital intercourse, passionate kissing should be defined as a problem. Necking is easier to control than are activities later in the behavior chain, and it is definitely a part of the sequence of behaviors leading to fornication.

Personal power is enhanced if you understand factors related to unwanted behavior and if you try to change your behavior at a point in the behavior chain at which you are most likely to be successful.

You Can Change Your World, to Some Extent

Assuming that you have identified the real problem, your next step is to develop potential solutions. Of course, this chapter concentrates on problems in environment, whereas other chapters talk about problems in other areas. In terms of external environment, there are essentially four ways in which you can neutralize the impact of cues related to unacceptable behavior. Such cues can be avoided, eliminated, or diluted. The fourth option is to add new factors to the situation. Explanation and examples of each option are given below.

Stay Away From Negative Influences

Merely staying away from factors associated with undesired behavior sounds simple, but usually it isn't. Sometimes exposure to the factor is necessary in daily living; for example, the behavior of a child may be related to his mother's loss of temper, yet avoiding the child altogether is not a practical solution for her. Such situations call for a little creativity. "Time out" or forced isolation for the child when he behaves unacceptably is an excellent discipline technique. Not only does it usually get the point across to the child, but it also can help you avoid exposure to the behavior that is upsetting you.

You can't avoid going to work, as a rule. But if your work is associated with a particular bad habit, you can often avoid placing yourself in certain situations at work that cue the undesired habit. You might try avoiding the cafeteria or staying away from vending machines, for instance. In short, even though certain situations can't always be totally avoided, there are ways of avoiding those aspects of a situation that are particularly relevant cues to bad habits. Personal research is often the best way of identifying what those aspects are.

Even when you can avoid cues to unwanted behavior, they are sometimes so pleasurable that you don't want to give them up. Substitution is a possibility where this is the case. Helen substituted radio for television as background to her work. The young people who find extended kissing pleasurable can pool their ideas for activities that they could both enjoy but that would not cue sexual involvement. Where substitution is impractical, and where sexual problems are not the issue, it is sometimes possible to place the pleasant cue after, rather than before, the undesired behavior—i.e., watching television, but only after progress toward a particular goal has been made. Ideas in this area are given in chapter 7 on reinforcement.

Even though cues to inadequate behavior cannot always be avoided easily, the possibility should not be prematurely dismissed. You may have to take a longer route to work, but you can usually avoid passing the adult bookstore or the liquor store or the doughnut shop or other problem areas. Such avoidance is not likely to eliminate compulsive behavior, but why make it more difficult on yourself by creating additional temptation through unnecessary exposure to cues associated with the undesired activity?

Eliminate Cues to Unwanted Behavior

Obviously, it is easy to avoid cues or antecedents of undesired behaviors if they no longer exist. Of course, I am not recommending that you blow up the pornography shop or the liquor store, although you might work for laws to eliminate or at least reduce the visibility of such establishments. On the other hand, it may be reasonable to sell the television set if that is a problem; or you can alter whom you spend time with if particular people are associated with undesired activities. It might not be practical to cut off your fingers if you bite your nails, but you can stop resting your chin on your hand if that behavior is related to the habit. If overeating is a problem, refusing to buy irresistible foods is another way of eliminating cues from your environment.

As suggested above, it is sometimes difficult to eliminate factors related to unwanted behavior if they are themselves desirable activities. Of course, it may not be necessary to do away with positive cues forever. As an example, once a habit has been broken, it may be possible to return to the television, or to begin to read the newspaper again, without negative effect. Substituting and reversing the order of cues in your environment, as suggested above, is also a worthwhile strategy in dealing with inherently positive factors related to unwanted behavior.

Dilute Negative Influences

If a cue cannot be eliminated or avoided, it usually can at least be diluted. If cookies are a problem to the dieter, but a "necessity" to other family members, cookies can be purchased that are relatively unappealing to the dieter, and/or they can be put away out of sight. For general meals, small plates can be used to increase the relative size of portions served, and less appealing entrees can be prepared. The relevant question is, how can you change the factor related to the undesired activity in a way that lessens its influence?

Add Positive Factors to Your Environment

It is also useful to create cues that suggest and/or are related to positive actions. Some of the simplest cues available are signs or notes to yourself. These can be somewhat creative: A card saying "four pounds of ugly fat" might be prominently displayed in the refrigerator as a reminder of your weight goal. Or you might place simple index cards with reminders of your goal in various places throughout your environment (e.g., *Thin Is Beautiful*). Whatever reminds you of your goal and effectively serves as a cue for positive behavior toward that goal can be effective. This is obviously the idea behind President Kimball's good advice to display a picture of a temple prominently in the home.

Positive cues tend to lose their impact with continued exposure, so you need to move cues about and to change them regularly. You should also remember that people can serve as cues to certain behaviors. The age-old suggestion to choose friends wisely has been repeated over the years for good reason. It is important to spend time with individuals who do the things and have the values you are striving toward.

Environment Is Important

As suggested at the outset of this chapter, it is possible to improve yourself the hard way, but there is no special virtue in it. You need to research your environment and understand what factors influence your behavior. You can then creatively modify your environment so that cues work for rather than against you. Once factors influencing your behavior have been identified, ask yourself, how can I avoid, eliminate, or modify these factors? Also ask yourself, what can I add to my environment that will help me solve this problem?

Chapter 6

The Attitude Element: Personal Power From Inside Out

The previous chapter discussed how we can use our environment in developing personal power. Of course, there is also an internal environment to consider. Faith, incentive, and emotion are essential factors controlling our behavior, and each one is controlled by our thoughts. The private world of our attitudes, assumptions, and perceptions is therefore a critically important element in determining self-direction and growth.

Faith Results From the Way We Think

We are motivated to make certain choices because we assume that the options chosen will have some advantage for us. In effect, we have faith that doing something will work. You follow the steps involved in starting your car because you assume that turning the ignition key will do the job. Stated another way, you have faith that turning the key will start the car. You obey the Word of Wisdom because you assume that doing so results in a healthier body and a closer relationship with God. Essentially, you have faith in the Word of Wisdom. Notice that faith, at least at its simplest level, seems to be based on assumptions. What we think controls faith, and faith, or incentive, has a lot to do with the choices we make.

As pointed out earlier, having faith in ourselves is also an important element in motivation. You can have faith that a certain choice is in your best interest, but you must also assume that it is within your power to achieve it. For example, you can have great faith that you would look better and feel better if you lose weight. However, if you are convinced that you lack the self-discipline necessary, you will not get far on a weight-reduction program. Your behavior is controlled both by what you assume about the value of different choice options before you *and* by what you conclude about your abilities.

Emotion Is Controlled by What We Think

Emotion, like faith, also seems to be controlled by the way we think. Suppose that someone rudely cuts in front of you on the freeway. Most people would be somewhat irritated, but not everyone would become angry about it. On a good day, you might easily pass it off, but on a day when things have gone wrong, you are more likely to be angry. Since your emotions can vary so much in response to the same situation, the situation must not be causing the emotions. Rather, how you are thinking about the situation causes the emotion. It isn't hard to imagine how you would feel if you thought, "What a rude, careless jerk! I won't stand to be treated like that; I'll show him." On the other hand, thinking, "No use getting upset. I can't let his action ruin my day," would have a positive emotional outcome.

Jane has just left her husband. She is feeling a wide variety of emotions, ranging from anger to guilt to fear. Again, the fact of her divorce is not causing the emotion, but what she is thinking about it is. Sometimes her thinking centers on how unfair her husband is and how deeply he hurt her; the resulting emotion is anger. At other times Jane assumes that she probably did not work hard enough to save the marriage, and she concentrates on some of her personal failures in the relationship. Guilt results. At still other times, she may be thinking about how difficult the future will be, and she may entertain doubt about her ability to provide for herself and her children. Jane then becomes afraid. These and other emotions come and go, sometimes overlapping, *depending on what Jane is thinking at the time.*

Our Thought Patterns Are Sometimes Below Awareness

"As he thinketh in his heart, so is he" (Proverbs 23:7). As this proverb and the preceding comments suggest, behavior is largely directed by assumptions, attitude, and thought. It is therefore critical that the messages we send to ourselves be supportive of our goals. Guaranteeing this can be a problem, however, since we are not always aware of our mental processes. At times, our thoughts follow habitual patterns, operating either so rapidly or so routinely that they occur without our awareness.

Sherrie, for example, usually has an instantaneous reaction to a certain look from her husband. Her anger is cued so rapidly that it almost appears as if the look from her husband is causing her anger. Actually, Sherrie has had enough experience with her husband that seeing the look automatically leads her to certain conclusions: namely, that he is being critical, he has no business treating her that way, and she won't stand for it. Her anger would not occur in the absence of such preprogrammed thoughts.

Routine mental functioning can also occur without awareness. We can drive long distances performing intricate road maneuvers without giving direct thought to each operation. We also perform many other routine but very complex behaviors without much conscious thought, such as walking, eating, dressing ourselves, doing chores, and thousands of similar things. It seems that we also follow certain thought patterns without awareness; in effect, we make many decisions without consciously weighing alternatives. We respond automatically, depending on our preexisting attitudes and beliefs, as did Sherrie in the preceding example.

Of course, all of this is generally as it should be. The sheer number of decisions that need to be made in daily living and the sophisticated behavioral patterns necessary in normal functioning demand that we operate automatically in most cases. A problem exists, however, when our preprogrammed thinking is faulty. It is then necessary for us to dig out the thoughts involved and to bring them into awareness in order to change them. Following are some ideas regarding how to do this.

Become Aware of Thoughts Before and After Particular Behaviors

As suggested above, we have so many thoughts about so many different things that it becomes difficult to monitor our internal processes in order to discover counterproductive thinking. Adding to the difficulty immensely is the fact that much of what we think occurs without our awareness. One strategy that can help is to focus on what you are thinking at specific times. If you are trying to change a particular behavior, it is important that you know what you were thinking just before and just after each instance of the behavior in question. The most direct way of finding this out is simply to ask yourself what you must have been thinking at the time. If you can't do this informally in your head, try the more formal paper-and-pencil approaches described below.

Method 1: Formal Thought Assessment

After each incident of the behavior you want to change, ask yourself two questions: "What do I remember thinking at the time?" and "What must I have been thinking in order to feel and act the way I did?" These questions will normally reveal the important thought patterns involved. Record what comes to mind as suggested below. (This record was made by someone attempting to quit smoking.)

Time	Quantity	Thinking
8:30 A.M.	(cigarettes)	(B — before smoking)

Time	Quantity	Thinking
	1	(A — after smoking)

(B) I can't keep my cool during the meeting if I don't smoke.

(B) People are going to think I'm a witch if I don't smoke.

(B) I can't quit; I've tried before.

(B) There are more important things than not smoking.

(A) You idiot! You blew it!

(A) That wasn't necessary. You could have gone without smoking.

(A) Jerry's going to be so disappointed in me.

(A) I'm kidding myself. I can't stop.

If this individual kept a similar record for each cigarette he smoked, the problems in his thinking would become obvious. Even though only one instance of smoking is recorded in the example above, it is apparent that thinking led directly to the decision to smoke, and self-condemnation occurred afterward, robbing the individual of an opportunity to learn what went wrong and chipping away at his self-confidence. He will likely continue to smoke as long as such thinking habits continue.

Method 2: After-the-Fact Recordings

Jim wants to share the gospel with his friends, but he doesn't. Even though he is not totally aware of the assumptions he makes, some of them are as follows:

—Other people will think I am a religious fanatic if I push the Church.

—Other people will be offended by invitations to religious thought or activity.

—I don't know enough about the gospel to explain it to others.

—People make too many demands if I get close to them.

—I don't spend enough time with my kids already.

—There is only one right, best way to approach people about
the Church.

These assumptions lead to specific conclusions and a decision
against proselyting when opportunities arise. For instance, while
missionaries were visiting with Jim and his family, it occurred to
Jim that a particular neighbor, Bob, might be interested in the
Church. Once the thought was registered, it was filtered through
Jim's attitudes and assumptions. The resulting conclusions (again
largely below the awareness level) were:

—I would lose Bob's respect and friendship if I brought up the
Church.

—Bob would feel obligated to appear interested, but he really
wouldn't be.

—Bob would ask questions that I couldn't answer.

—I have too many family pressures right now to spend time
on this.

—If I got closer to Bob, he would probably be bugging me all
the time.

—I should wait for a better time. It's a good idea, but the timing isn't right.

After the missionaries left, Jim thought about contacting his
neighbor but soon put the idea out of his mind as he went on to
other things. Jim was not really aware of it, but he reached his
decision based on the thinking described above. The decision
was basically an automatic one, made without a lot of conscious
thought and with only a vague understanding of the factors considered in the decision.

To uncover what his thinking and conclusions were, Jim had
to stop and work backward. "I must have made a decision not to
contact Bob. I wonder what I was thinking that led to that conclusion?" Jim then wrote down what came to mind in answer to
this question. (Simply doing this in his head would not have
been as effective as using paper and pencil.) This process resulted
in identifying much of the thinking described above. From there,
it was a matter of guessing what underlying general assumptions
he must have had that led to such conclusions..

Method 3: Random Recordings

The strategies outlined above are useful when you are trying to break a habit, or to uncover mental obstacles in the way of some desired activity. But, at times, you may desire to gain a more general awareness of your thought habits. Dan, for example, wanted to become less self-critical. Since self-criticism is itself a thought process, it was necessary for Dan to monitor his thoughts in general. In order to do this, Dan distributed red index cards in his environment in places that he would come across during his daily routine—one in his lunch sack, one on the dashboard of his car, one on his calendar at work, one by his tennis racket, one on his workbench, and one by his toothbrush.

Whenever he came across an index card he asked himself how he was feeling and what he had been thinking in the preceding few minutes. If he was not aware of thinking much of anything, he worked backward from his feelings. "I'm feeling depressed. What must I have been thinking to cause me to feel this way?" Dan simply made a mental note of his observations, although recording his notes on paper would have been much more effective. From his mental note taking, Dan became aware of a lot of self-condemning and counterproductive thinking. With awareness, he had a necessary key in hand to do something about it.

How to Change Counterproductive Thought Habits

Dan, in the previous example, found that he merely had to become aware of his self-critical thinking in order to reduce it. Once he tuned in to his self-criticism, he was able to tune it out. In fact, awareness is often all that we need in order to fix problems in our thinking. At other times we may have to undertake a more formal attitude-change program.

Jim's problem with proselyting referred to earlier required an active attitude-change effort. Essentially, he evaluated each of his conclusions and assumptions on the basis of two questions: "Is it really true?" and "Does the thought help me reach my goal?" His answers to these questions are given below. It became obvious that all of his assumptions and conclusions contradicted his proselyting goal, and they were also based on faulty logic.

Assumption: Other people will think I am a religious fanatic if I push religion.

It depends on what I do. I am not planning to behave in extreme ways. Certainly, simple invitations to religious discussions or events will not lead right-thinking people to label me a fanatic. Anyway, I don't care to be friends with the few people who would think so. I don't think less of others who communicate a religious conviction. Others won't think less of me.

Assumption: Other people will be offended by invitations to religious thought or activity.

Other people will be offended only if I push them or if I am not genuinely interested in them. I am not going to push and I am genuinely interested; therefore, there is no problem. Others are pleased, not offended, by expressions of interest in them.

Assumption: I don't know enough about the gospel to explain it to others.

I know that I am interested in the gospel, and that is all that is necessary for me to invite someone else to learn along with me. I don't have to have all the answers. An "I don't know, but I'll find out" comment is always appropriate. Besides, I do know a lot more about the gospel than nonmembers do, and I do know that it is true.

Assumption: Missionary work would take too much time away from my family.

I need to spend more time with the family, but I don't have to sacrifice missionary work for time with the kids. In fact, I can include them in different ways; I could invite Bob and his family to join in home evenings or other activities with my family and me.

Assumption: People make too many demands if I get close to them. This is not universally true. I don't expect Bob to be a problem. Even if he is, I can always say no. I am in charge of the degree of commitment I make to the relationship. I have nothing to fear.

Assumption: There is only one right, best way to approach people about the Church.

My approach and timing don't have to be perfect. I need to care and to make the effort. I can leave the rest up to the Lord.

Once Jim decided that his assumptions were not correct and, in fact, contradicted his goal, he changed them to the following:

—No one will think I am a fanatic. I am not unreasonable.

—I won't offend anyone by showing an interest in them.

—I don't have to know everything about the gospel to be effective.

—I don't have to sacrifice time with the kids for missionary work.

—I can control any demands of a relationship with Bob.

—I don't have to wait for the ideal time and approach.

The process up to this point was helpful, but Jim still felt afraid and was reluctant to approach others about the Church. Even though he was convinced of the truth of his new list of assumptions, he still tended to think the old way. It was therefore necessary for him to give the new way of thinking more emphasis. He did this by memorizing the new list of assumptions and repeating them in his mind many times a day over the course of a few days. Emphatically repeating the new thoughts helped Jim to replace the old assumptions. Jim felt awkward about this procedure and it seemed to be a futile exercise at first. But he persisted, and there came a point at which the new assumptions took hold and began to influence his thinking and behavior as certainly as did the old.

Having a Correct Philosophy of Life

Not only must we learn how to monitor and control our thinking in day-to-day situations, but to gain full personal power we must operate on correct principles in our general philosophy of life. We need to be certain, for example, that assumptions and attitudes by which we operate our life are rooted in gospel principles, such as honesty, morality, and service. Other attitudes of particular relevance in developing personal power are, of course, suggested throughout this book. For emphasis, several of these attitudes are summarized below.

Attitude 1: I Can Do It!

I can't do everything. I can't climb every mountain or ford every stream. I can't learn everything there is to know about everything during my life. I can't be a concert pianist, a world renowned artist, or a professional basketball player. I am lacking the necessary talent to do some things, and the time and energy to do others. But I can learn to direct myself. I can learn to make productive choices consistently (remembering that saying "no" to some service requests and choosing to relax are oftentimes productive choices), and I can learn to manage my emotions effectively.

Personal power is not an inborn trait, but a skill that can be developed. To some people, this power sometimes seems impossible to obtain, but that feeling results because (1) they are not going about the task in the correct way, or (2) they are creating obstacles for themselves in their thinking and in their external environment. It really is possible to develop personal power, and it doesn't necessarily take a long time. Power to direct specific behaviors can come quickly if approached in the proper way. Of course, obtaining ultimate personal power and total self-direction ability is a lifetime pursuit.

Attitude 2: I Am a Person of Worth Even Though I Am Not Perfect

As suggested earlier, many people are afraid to accept their own inherent worth because they assume that this will rob them of motivation to overcome their weaknesses. Actually, motivation to improve is lost only when we decide that our conduct isn't so bad after all—which is the natural progression of things once we lose faith in our ability to direct our behavior.

It's easier for us to accept ourselves if we remember that good people do bad things occasionally. You can respect your spirit and your potential even if your behavior is not totally respectable. Drawing the distinction between the worth of the behavior and the worth of the soul helps protect your self-confidence while you are yet growing. It also builds your faith in your ability to improve, which is so necessary in effective self-direction. The Apostle Peter was a person of worth and infinite potential even though he was apparently impetuous and perhaps even cowardly at one point in his life. You and I are also beings of infinite worth and potential even though we are not yet perfected.

Attitude 3: It Helps to Change My Environment

Developing personal power isn't easy if we attempt to change a behavior while at the same time continuing to be exposed to all the environmental cues related to it. You could hardly get comfortable with public speaking if you were continually telling yourself how frightening it was and how you would probably make a fool out of yourself. Changing either the world around you or your thoughts (or both, preferably) can make the job much easier, and there is no virtue in this case in doing it the hard way.

There often is virtue in doing certain things the hard way. We voted for the hard way when the plan for mortality was established. Someone who is given everything often loses the many advantages of having to work for what he gets. But it really is a different situation when it comes to self-direction. In building personal power, the easiest way is usually the best way—and often it is the only way.

Attitude 4: It Doesn't Hurt to Reinforce Myself

Somewhere along the line people often pick up the notion that it is wrong for them to recognize the good they do. This tendency probably has its roots in concern about avoiding pride. "Only the proud, egotistical individual would go around complimenting himself," we think. In fact, a proud, egotistical person often does compliment himself publicly, and he is anxious to take credit for the positive and refuse responsibility for the negative. On the other hand, *private* recognition of accomplishment avoids the "egotist" problem and helps you build confidence in your ability to reach legitimate goals. When you appreciate yourself privately, you have less need to do it publicly.

Tricia is like many individuals who feel inadequate and who assume that their behavior is not praiseworthy. When asked if she had accomplished anything in the last twenty-four hours, she said no. When she analyzed her activities hour by hour, however, it became obvious that she had made many correct choices and had actually been quite productive. Her problem was a reluctance to recognize accomplishment and to appreciate herself.

There is nothing wrong with (in fact there is something very right about) complimenting yourself for successes and recognizing the good you do. This is true even if your successes are not spectacular and even if you do some things poorly. Rather than hold you back, such reinforcement can enhance productivity.

Attitude 5: I Can Handle Success

Many seem to make progress toward a goal, but then find that they give up trying. This often occurs because they fear what will happen if improvement is made. Janet is considerably overweight in spite of frequent weight-loss attempts. Janet's main problem is that she is afraid to be thin. Janet has a history of disturbed relationships with men, and she is deathly afraid of being hurt again. Overweight is an important feature of Janet's defense system against rejection; until she can give up her fear of losing weight, Janet is not likely to have much success with her diet programs.

Others are afraid of success for other reasons, which commonly boil down to a fear of being successful now because more will be expected later. "If I am successful in school I might get locked into a job I can't handle." "If I say the prayer in class, I will be asked to give a talk in sacrament meeting." In general, it is not uncommon for individuals to hold themselves back from something they know they could accomplish for fear it would lead to something they would almost certainly fail at.

Attitude 6: I Don't Have to Try Too Hard

If a goal is an important one, a person often becomes overly concerned about reaching it. He may be successful in spite of his intensity, but excessive concern is usually counterproductive. Some of the reasons why this is so were identified earlier. They include cueing the problem by thinking too much about it, putting oneself down when progress is slower than desired, and creating destructive emotions rather than focusing on learning.

When a person is stuck in the mud, it makes little sense for him to panic and "give it the gas." Spinning wheels dig deeper into the mud. Slow, even pressure is more likely to be successful, particularly if the driver precedes it by placing a few sticks or rocks in the tread path for traction. When we undertake self-improvement projects, slow, even progress is again the best procedure. It also helps if we work with our external and internal environments in order to gain the traction needed.

Attitude 7: I Can Depend on the Lord's Help

An earlier chapter emphasizes the divine help that is available to us as we attempt to build personal power. When we have temporary power failures, the shortages can be made up by the Lord, assuming that we are willing and able to utilize his help.

The Lord has suggested that his servants are also his friends (D&C 84:77). The thought of having a member of the Godhead as a personal friend is appealing. What could there be to fear under that circumstance? How confident we could be of our ability to grow and become stronger! Just being aware that the Lord's support was available would be tremendously helpful. Suppose that you were asked to walk along a beam one foot wide which was lying on the ground. You could probably do so confidently and efficiently. Now suppose the same beam were suspended a thousand feet above the ground. You would no doubt falter and perhaps fall. When life's circumstances become frightening, having Christ's support available is like knowing that the beam rests on the ground.

Let's Control Our Thinking

The foundation of effective self-direction is found in gospel principles and in attitudes such as those reviewed here. Some of the best ways of insuring that the principles by which we govern our lives are correct have been identified by prophets from the beginning. They include studying the scriptures, being faithful and active in the Church, and praying meaningfully.

Insuring that your life philosophy is correct is accomplished by living the gospel. You can change counterproductive thoughts and guarantee that you have a positive mental environment by following the three steps that were outlined above: (1) discover the pattern of thought that controls your behavior; (2) see if these thoughts can be changed to ones that are supportive of your personal goals; and (3) memorize and repeat the new attitudes constantly until it has become a habit to think the new way. Since attitudes and thoughts are the key to self-direction, it is critically important that you learn to control them. Personal power is directly correlated with the extent to which we effectively manage our attitudes and thoughts.

Chapter 7

The Reinforcement Element in Personal Power

Along with the ideas already discussed, you can increase personal power by rewarding yourself for performing desired behavior. Both scientific research and common sense suggest that if something we do leads to a positive outcome, we will repeat it if possible. If something we do leads to a negative consequence, we will tend to avoid it in the future. Of course, with humans this tendency isn't always straightforward. What is positive for some people is negative for others; people like different kinds of food, music, and literature. Some people will endure great pain and physical discomfort in the short run in order to reap long-term benefits. Others will suffer in the long run in order to have comfort at the moment.

Even so, the fact remains that the consequences of our behavior have a lot to do with the choices we make. We need, therefore, to insure that we associate desired behaviors with positive consequences and that undesired behaviors are related to negative outcomes. Making these associations is referred to as *reinforcement strategy*. Again, this doesn't always happen naturally. You will probably have to put forth some effort to structure your environment in the manner suggested.

For example, suppose that your goal is to increase your level of exercise. Unless you are one of the few who (for some inexplicable reason) find the short-term pain and discomfort of exercise programs rewarding, a little environmental engineering is in order. You need to do something to increase the positive and lessen the negative short-term effects of exercising for yourself.

Three Primary Strategies for Rewarding Yourself

There are at least three general options for rewarding yourself that will be illustrated in this chapter. The first is to pair something positive with the desired behavior. With respect to exercising, this could be accomplished by listening to your favorite music over radio headphones as you're jogging, by walking with a good friend, or by exercising through competitive sports (if you enjoy this). Positives could also follow the activity. Scheduling newspaper reading, listening to music, eating breakfast, or enjoying some other favorite activity immediately after exercising will help reinforce the otherwise negative exercise experience, especially if the favorite activity is made contingent on completing exercise plans. Obviously, self-congratulation for having exercised and the good feelings involved can be reinforcing; but many of us need more than that.

Another general option is to pair something negative with the undesired behavior. Using the exercise example, failing to follow your exercise regimen is what you are trying to avoid. Not allowing yourself to read the newspaper if exercise has not been completed, or giving your wife five dollars to spend on herself for every day you procrastinate are examples of pairing something negative with the undesired behavior. (Note the point made earlier that self-criticism is not very effective as punishment for not doing something you should. The impact of criticism on self-esteem as well as other consequences suggest against its use.)

A third general option is to increase the immediate relevance of the long-term positives associated with a desired activity. Virtually everything that someone is motivated to do has a long-term benefit to the individual. The problem is that, as with the exercising example, the long-term benefit of many activities is decidedly long-term. In the short run, there are often more enjoyable activities that compete with what we ought to do, and/or what we ought to do is itself uncomfortable for various reasons. Several strategies exist for increasing the relevance of long-term benefits. You can imagine yourself having already achieved the goal and try to visualize the benefits and good feelings involved. Or you can put cues in your environment that remind you of your goal, such as notes to yourself or pictures. You could imagine yourself thinner and feeling better because of sticking to an exercise program. You might also put your running shoes out where you will trip over them in the morning, or put up pictures of people who look and feel the way you expect to once you reach your goal. Whatever brings the goal into the present can be helpful.

In general, rewarding ourselves for desired behavior can be very helpful, but often we don't take advantage of this option in developing personal power.

Why Don't We Reward Ourselves More Often?

Virtually all of the reinforcement strategies that might be employed share one common drawback: They all have to be employed. Where desired reinforcement patterns occur naturally, there is little motivation problem. If an individual finds all aspects of exercising enjoyable, he typically will not have a problem sticking to such a program. Most of us, however, need to structure our environment to aid us in reaching our desired goals. Unfortunately, strategies for doing so all involve unnatural manipulation of our environment—which means that these approaches may add to the unpleasantness of a task or activity already disliked: "If I have to go out and buy radio earphones, write notes to myself, or follow any of the other suggestions, it just adds to the hassle."

Somehow we have to get motivated to do the things that will help us get motivated. This is easier, of course, if the reinforcement strategy selected is not expensive, in time or money. Part of the secret, then, is to select the right reinforcement program. We must also be convinced that rewarding ourselves is worth the trouble.

Another reason we sometimes don't bother to reinforce ourselves has to do with the "doing-it-the-hard-way-is-better" philosophy discussed earler. Some individuals are convinced that they are weak willed if they don't motivate themselves with strength of mind only (whatever that is). Doing this is like digging a swimming pool with a pick and shovel rather than a bulldozer. It may be possible to do it the hard way, but it doesn't make sense to avoid using all of the tools available simply because they make the job easier. The sensible approach is to understand the many factors affecting motivation and then to create a situation in which self-direction is most easily obtained.

A third obstacle to employing reinforcement strategies was also alluded to earlier. Some people feel guilty when they do nice things for themselves, or they fear that it will inhibit their *natural* desire to do well. This problem makes self-reinforcement programs difficult, since whatever positive thing might be done contributes to guilt. The guilt in turn obviously neutralizes the advantage of any reinforcement plan and dilutes its ability to help the individual achieve his goal.

What's Wrong With Using Reinforcement Programs?

What is so wrong with rewarding ourselves? Parents sometimes hesitate to reward their children for desired behavior out of fear that their offspring will not develop natural interest in correct behavior. In effect, these parents fear that their children will learn to respond only *if* rewards are offered. Children raised in this manner often have the same fear when working with themselves.

Actually, however, doing things only if rewarded already seems to be a fundamental feature of motivation for all of us. Not too many people would go to work if they were not paid on a regular basis. We would not do many of the things we do in the Church if the Lord had not specified very real advantages in our doing them.

In fact, the scriptures carefully point out the rewards of correct living and the negative consequences of sin. Very express language is used by the Lord on occasion, "that it might work upon the hearts of the children of men, altogether for my name's glory" (see D&C 19:6-12). In this regard, one assignment of the Holy Ghost appears to be to help us feel good about righteous choices and bad about unrighteous ones.

Taken in this light, reinforcement seems to be a universal thing. Our motivation and effectiveness in living increase as we let ourselves feel good about accomplishments and as we engineer into our lives positive rewards for desired behavior.

Step 1: Determine What Is Reinforcing

If we agree that reinforcement strategies are appropriate motivation builders, the next question is, how do we use them? First, we must gain an understanding of how to select reinforcers. Of course, an effective reinforcement strategy must be personalized. What will work under one circumstance might not under another. Take a few minutes and make a list of things that you truly enjoy. These should be activities that you find inherently satisfying, that is, activities that you look forward to and participate in without any sense of "I must" or "I have to." You might also identify possessions that you would enjoy owning but don't have. Your list might look something like the accompanying one, only with detail added. You should, for example, add specifics such as exactly what you like to read for pleasure, what music you prefer listening to, which friend you especially enjoy talking to, and so on.

One obvious criterion of a successful reinforcer is that it have value to the person involved. Making a list of valued activities and possessions can help you identify several potential reinforcers that meet this criterion. Additionally, a personal reinforcer should be relatively simple to implement. Even a valued activity such as playing golf may not be an effective reinforcer if it involves schedule problems, a long drive to the course, battling the elements, and so forth. When employing a reinforcer, you must also be convinced that *you* are worth it. If you promise yourself a vacation for reaching a weight goal, but know you can't afford the trip and would feel guilty about going, the promised trip will not be an effective motivator.

Activity	*Possessions Would Like*
sports	new clothes
reading for relaxation	books
listening to music	records
talking to a friend	sports equipment
taking a nap	recreation equipment
taking a walk	hobby equipment
meditating	work-saving devices
eating	
hobbies	
television	
games	
trips	
boating	

Another important feature of a personal reinforcer is that it be something that can be added to your routine regularly. The promise of a new wardrobe if a weight goal is met or the offer of a new car for graduating from school can be effective in some cases, but typically such rewards are too far removed in time from the behavior involved in reaching the goal. Less expensive, easier-to-implement rewards such as pleasure reading, television watching, or taking a brief nap immediately after desired behavior are sometimes better. Of course, there is no reason you cannot include both types of rewards in your reinforcement program.

Step 2: Specify Behavior You Want to Change

No matter what reinforcer you select, a reinforcement plan cannot be implemented until you have defined the specific behavior you want to develop or eliminate. This usually is not as simple as it may sound. Suppose, for instance, that your goal is to be less critical. What does that mean? You may call something a suggestion, but your spouse calls it criticism. You may not say anything at all but communicate criticism nonverbally by a look or some action you take. There is also the distinction between critical thought and critical action to consider. In order to employ a reinforcement program you need to define what you consider to be a critical act precisely enough so that you can recognize and label such acts consistently when they occur.

Suppose your goal is to get better grades. Again, the behaviors involved are complex. Class attendance, paying attention in class, turning work in on time, spending adequate amounts of time in study, and a whole series of specific study habits are involved. Since a reinforcement program could be developed to improve any of these specific behaviors, the exact behavior(s) you want to reinforce must be defined. You could simply reward yourself at the end of the semester for getting good grades, but again, it is usually better to reinforce specific actions along the way toward the goal. In any event, the behavior you intend to reinforce needs to be defined exactly so that you will consistently be able to tell whether it has occurred or not.

In defining the behavior you want to reinforce, it helps to think through all of the steps along the way to goal achievement. Behaviors most often procrastinated or most difficult to complete are the prime candidates for reinforcement. Research like that described in chapter 4 may help you identify where reinforcement is needed.

Step 3: Implement a Reinforcement Plan

Once you have a list of potential reinforcers, and you know the behaviors you wish to reinforce, you are in a position to begin pairing reinforcers with desired behavior.

Pair Positive Outcomes With Desired Behavior

As described earlier, one general method in reinforcement planning is to follow desired behavior with positives. As examples of what can be done, following are several goals and possible reinforcement strategies. Again, in order to be effective, what you do must be tailored to your personal situation. If in reviewing these examples you find the concept of rewarding behavior to be objectionable, refer again to the arguments given earlier in favor of reinforcement strategies.

Goal: To get better grades in school (sixteen-year-old).
Reinforcement Strategy: Get your parents to agree to pay you ten dollars for every A in academic subjects at the end of the semester. On arriving home from school, don't eat anything except in your study room. Take a snack to your desk, and eat it before your study period (as reinforcement for deciding to study). Follow every thirty to forty-five minutes of study with fifteen minutes of a favorite activity, such as listening to music or talking with a friend. Don't allow yourself to become involved in favorite activities until you have completed a set amount of study. And limit your "favorite activity" time to what you have allotted yourself.

Goal: To yell at the kids less.
Reinforcement Strategy: Keep a record of yelling incidents by day (simple tally sheet). Give yourself one hour of an activity you enjoy but don't often make the time for—such as pleasure reading, doing a hobby, listening to music—for every three-hour block of time in which you have not yelled at the kids. If caring for the children or other duties make this impossible, reward yourself with a babysitter and a night out for every day you refrain from yelling.

Goal: To lose weight.
Reinforcement Strategy: Dish up reasonable portions at meals, and let yourself enjoy a favorite activity afterward if you eat only the portions served. Reward yourself with a favorite activity for going one hour (or more) without a snack after the thought first occurs and the desire to snack is strong. Offer yourself a new wardrobe, vacation, or some other prize for obtaining your weight goal on schedule.

As suggested at the outset, these examples apply to specific situations and are meant only to illustrate the potential use of reinforcement strategies. Someone with a weight problem obviously should not use snacks as a reinforcer for study habits (as in the first example). Also, a reinforcer should not be so inherently attractive that it interferes with goal achievement. Using the study example, under some circumstances, talking with a friend for a few minutes would be an effective reward after a study period. Under other circumstances, the conversation might be difficult to break away from, or a friend may suggest activities that interfere with study. Common sense and a little experimenting should lead to an effective reinforcement program in any individual situation.

In the second example (yelling at children), the time interval before allowing the reward was established on the basis of the incidence of yelling and on the demands of this individual's schedule. In general, the time interval between behavior and reward should not be so long that earning the reward is very difficult, nor so short that the reward comes too easily. Then, too, the interval may need to change as progress is made toward the goal. One night out for every day that yelling does not occur may be appropriate during the early stages of a behavior-change program, but may be excessive once going a day without yelling is easily achieved.

In all three examples, a question arises as to how long you should continue a pattern of reinforcement. The simple answer is, as long as it takes. The object is to reinforce behavior until habit patterns are established. At that point, most behavior will be self-reinforcing. Keep in mind also that things frequently enjoyed tend to lose value. You may find it helpful to vary reinforcers by picking several activities from your list of favorites and then using them alternatively.

Pair Negative Outcomes With Undesired Behavior

A second general option in reinforcement planning is to associate negative consequences with behaviors that contradict goal achievement. Two variations of this approach are (1) to take away something you like when undesired behavior occurs, or (2) to give yourself something you don't like. Assume that your goal is to stop swearing. Giving away a dollar bill or foregoing some enjoyed activity every time you swear are examples of the first possibility. Pulling a rubber band against your wrist sharply or doing some chore you dislike after every swearing incident are examples of the second. The idea is to pair something unpleasant with a behavior that is unwanted.

Punishment of this type can be helpful in reducing the incidence of unwanted behaviors, but, of course, it is often more difficult to motivate yourself to self-punish than to self-reward. In order to overcome this difficulty, you can get a family member or close friend to administer the negative consequence whenever he witnesses the undesired behavior. But that is not recommended if you want to stay friends! Somehow it doesn't sound like good relationship building to have your spouse shoot you with a rubber band every time you swear. Having others administer punishments also means that immediate reinforcement is often not possible (unless the other is with you *continually* for twenty-four hours a day). Then, too, externally provided punishment often leads one to avoid the punisher rather than the undesired behavior.

Don't give up on the idea too quickly, however. The general notion is sound, and it is a tool you don't want to ignore. Take a minute and complete the inverse of your list of favorite activities. Indicate activities you really dislike, along with possessions you would hate to give up. Your list may look something like the accompanying one. (Of course, this list obviously reflects only one person's attitudes and values. You may find some of these activities highly rewarding.

From the list of disliked activities you can select items to pair with undesired behaviors. Of course, denying yourself favorite activities (from the list previously prepared) or giving up a valued possession is another option when pairing negatives with unwanted behavior.

It isn't necessary from a reinforcement standpoint, but it makes sense to let negatives you add to your life be productive ones where possible. A despised food, for example, is probably good for you physically. Hated chores normally have value when completed. Possessions you decide to give up can obviously be given to someone in need rather than destroyed. The fact that the negative activity has a positive outcome probably will not detract from its usefulness as punishment for unwanted behavior.

Distasteful Activities	*Favorite Possessions*
cleaning the bathroom	favorite clothes
washing the car	jewelry
jogging, calisthenics	books
listening to opera	records
shopping	sports equipment
standing in lines	recreation equipment
babysitting someone else's	hobby equipment
children	work-saving devices
gardening	
eating bananas, spinach	
spending money	

You should remember, however, the need for the negative consequence to be paired with, or to follow closely, the undesired behavior. An advantage of giving up a dollar bill when swearing occurs is that it can follow immediately the undesired behavior. If you decide to donate a dollar you should have an envelope handy, and ceremoniously place a dollar in it at the time you swear. Of course, the dollar should also be in addition to any donation that you would make under normal circumstances.

Following are three goals and examples of how ideas suggested above can be applied. As with previous examples, these are intended to be illustrations only of the general approach. What you do needs to be personalized. It is also important to monitor the results of your reinforcement strategy. If, in fact, the incidence of unwanted behavior does not diminish significantly, a different reinforcement plan should be developed.

Goal: To reduce the incidence of criticizing your spouse.
Reinforcement Strategy: Eat a banana or other despised food after each instance of criticism, alternated (for the sake of your waist-

line) with ten pushups or a disliked chore from a prearranged list. As suggested earlier, this plan depends on an operational definition of critical interactions. Criteria must be developed by which you can evaluate your behavior and consistently determine what is and what is not critical behavior.

Goal: To get to sleep without tossing and turning.
Reinforcement Strategy: If worry and fret on retiring make it difficult for you to fall asleep, try the following procedure. Step 1: Place a clock so that it is visible from your bed. Step 2: If you have not fallen asleep in ten minutes, get out of bed and do ten pushups (more if pushups are easy for you). The longer you take, the better. Rest if necessary in between, but complete all the pushups. *All the while you are doing the pushups, make yourself think about the subjects that were going through your mind during the previous ten minutes in bed.* Step 3: Go back to bed for another ten minutes. Step 4: If you have not fallen asleep by the end of the second ten-minute interval, repeat the procedure.

The object of this approach is to pair something negative (pushups on a cold floor in the middle of the night) with sleep-robbing thoughts. The probability of worry then goes down, and the probability of falling asleep goes up. Notice that in this example, reinforcement principles can help in controlling your thoughts (internal behavior) as well as your actions (external behavior).

Keep in mind that this suggestion, like others in this book, works for some people but not for others. Some may find, for example, a stimulating effect from exercise that contradicts the potential benefit described above. Of course, whether this technique will help in your case remains to be seen until you try it.

Goal: To stop biting fingernails.
Reinforcement Strategy: Every time you bite your nails, place a dollar bill in an envelope for later donation to a worthy cause. Snap a rubber band against your wrist every time you notice your fingers close to your mouth. (The dollar amounts are suggestions only. You should choose a reasonable amount, consider-

ing your personal budget, but also an amount you would hate to part with.)

Pairing negatives with undesired behavior can be helpful, especially when included with other techniques. Several different approaches to self-management mentioned in this book are brought to bear on selected self-improvement goals in the last chapter.

Increase the Present Impact of a Long-Range Goal

Payoff from some important goals is delayed; that's just the way life is. The advantages of getting an education, for instance, usually come only after years of effort. In order to keep interest and motivation up, previous suggestions have dealt with creating reinforcers along the way toward goal achievement. It is also valuable to bring the advantages of obtaining long-term goals into the present. To some extent this can be done by creating cues or reminders of the goal, as explained in chapter 5. Another technique is to imagine goal achievement ahead of actually obtaining it.

Suppose that your goal is to marry in the temple. Between here and there you will typically experience a number of temptations, choices that may be pleasant at the moment, but that contradict temple standards. Pictures of the temple in your living quarters, regular interviews with parents or priesthood authorities, baptisms for the dead, a visit to a temple, scripture study, Church meetings, and Church service all provide useful cues and reminders of the desired goal. It also helps to imagine yourself having achieved the goal. Get a picture of a sealing room in one of the temples. Now, in daydream fashion, close your eyes and imagine yourself and someone you love kneeling at that altar. Inventing as much detail as possible, imagine the touch of hands across the altar, the warm embrace with loved ones after the ceremony. Imagine how you feel inside. Let yourself enjoy that moment to the fullest.

You may find that this imagery experience works best if you pretend that you are watching the whole experience on television or at the movies. Look at yourself and at the others present.

Imagine how everyone is dressed and how everyone looks. Look at the tears of satisfaction and joy from those who care about you as the ceremony progresses. Let yourself feel the acceptance and loving support of the Lord.

This exercise, repeated occasionally, can help to bring some of the emotional benefits of achieving long-term goals into the present. No matter what the specific goal is, let yourself mentally experience the joy of reaching your objective. Imagine the benefit to you, the reaction of others, and let yourself feel, to the extent possible, the general satisfaction you expect from the goal's achievement.

Thoughts Also Reinforce Behavior

Chapter 6 dealt at length with the issue of how important our thoughts are in controlling how we feel and act. The issue is brought up again here as a reminder that giving yourself verbal compliments can help reinforce goal-directed activity. In addition to external rewards, we need to pair positive thought with desired behavior.

Larry is attempting to control his temper. He came home from work one evening to pandemonium. The kids were running amok, his wife was harried, dinner was late, and what he found was generally not at all the peaceful, happy experience he had anticipated. Larry struggled with himself but essentially handled the situation without blowing up. After order had been restored and he had some time to himself, Larry became aware of the following thoughts running through his mind:

— "You idiot, you almost blew it!"
— "Why can't you be calm and collected when you come home?"
— "You're going to louse up your marriage and family the way it's going."
— "Why can't Linda control the kids better?"

Larry overlooked the fact that he had handled the situation fairly well and instead emphasized what might have happened. He chose to feel bad that he wasn't perfectly calm in the situation, rather than to stress to himself that he didn't blow up, even with considerable provocation. In violation of the principles discussed above, Larry paired negative rather than positive thinking with the desired behavior (not blowing up). Following are more productive thoughts:

- —"I made it! I wasn't perfect, but I didn't blow up."
- —"I was reasonably calm and collected given the circumstances."
- —"I know I can do it! If I can handle tonight, I can handle anything."
- —"Even Linda had a problem. I think most anyone would."

In order to reinforce your effort, it is important that your conversations with yourself during and following desired behavior be positive. The opposite doesn't work very well, however: It normally is not a good idea to pair negative self-discussion with unwanted behavior. The impact of criticism on self-esteem, and its contribution to emotionalism rather than learning from mistakes, increases rather than decreases the probability of the undesired behavior recurring.

Recording Your Successes and Failures Can Be Motivating

Achievement and accomplishment are inherently satisfying to human beings under normal circumstances. Being right or correct is also naturally reinforcing. Simply recording accomplishments and failures can therefore be motivating. Chapter 5 gives examples of data-collection procedures for use when identifying factors related to specific behaviors. Similar charts and graphs are also helpful in reinforcing goal-directed behavior.

For example, Ruth had a weight problem. Personal research indicated that snacks between meals were a major problem for her. Ruth noted on paper the number of snacks she consumed each day over a one- to two-week period. She then used this information to change her environment in ways that made it easier for her to reduce snacking. By continuing to record the number of snacks consumed after she began her attempt to stop eating between meals, she made the record itself a reinforcer for nonsnacking behavior. Her graph showed a daily average consumption of eight snacks per day prior to her cut-off date, which went down to zero snacks for three days afterward. Marking a zero on the chart at the end of each of those days was rewarding. Ruth had three snacks on the fourth day, which she reluctantly recorded on her graph. Recording the three snacks was a negative experience for her (paired with the unwanted behavior of snacking). But looking at the still dramatic drop from eight snacks a day to three by the fourth day gave Ruth incentive (faith) to get back on her no-snacking program. She might otherwise have felt like a total failure for having had the three snacks, and then given up her goal in despair.

Many behaviors are amenable to this kind of recording. Like Ruth, you will generally find that the act of recording successes and failures along the way to goal achievement reinforces the behavior desired.

Public Commitment Is a Good Motivator

All of us want to be respected by others. Some of us want this more than we should, but we all want it to some degree. This means that we can use our concern about the respect of others as a reinforcer for goal-directed behavior. Self-improvement efforts are often most successful if undertaken publicly. If you are going to lose weight, make it a big issue socially. Pick a target date and then get the word out to friends and associates. Put your reputation on the line, and the chance of success will go up under most conditions.

If you are beginning an exercise regimen, you will usually have more success if you exercise with a friend. Having someone else work with you lessens the negative aspects of the activity. It also means that someone else is depending on you, which most of us find motivating. Many people are also motivated by competition. Competitive weight-loss programs or competitive study programs are sometimes more likely to be successful than individual efforts.

Public commitment and social reinforcement are generally of value, but you should be careful when family or close personal relationships are involved. A spouse's support of a self-improvement effort may come dangerously close to nagging. Likewise, the "here-you-go-again" response that you might get from your partner is hardly motivating. Depending on the kind of relationship you have, sometimes a spouse or close friend can help most by being uninvolved as you work toward a self-improvement goal.

Motivate Yourself to Get Motivated

Several of the many suggestions in this chapter may help you develop personal power. As indicated earlier, however, most of these suggestions involve manipulating your environment in some way, which is work! The danger is that you will be tempted to "save time and effort" by just trying to go ahead and solve the problem. That may be effective, but it is not recommended. Planning, preparation, and carefully directed effort are more likely to result in success.

Chapter 8

The Negative Element: Rationalizing Can Get in the Way

Previous chapters have talked about elements that we need to put in place when strengthening our personal power. This chapter discusses a factor that needs to be removed, or at least managed, if we are to be self-directed. This factor, rationalization, is a necessary, healthy aspect of coping with our world; however, at times it can also be an obstacle to reaching our goals.

It's Easy to Fool Ourselves

One of Aesop's fables has given us the expression "sour grapes." Once it became obvious to the fox that the delicious-looking cluster of grapes was out of his reach, he decided that the grapes were sour and that he didn't want them anyway. The fox then went on this way protected from the feeling of having failed to achieve something he wanted. You and I, of course, are sometimes tempted to do the same thing. "Practicing is too hard, but I really don't want to learn to play the piano anyway." "I can't seem to stick to an exercise program, but that's all right, because I feel fine." "She won't go out with me, but who wants her anyway? She is so stuck up."

The "sweet-lemon" reaction is an extension of the "sour-grapes" idea. According to the "sweet-lemon" notion, not only is the goal unattainable, but the present is remarkably satisfying. "I have so many things going for me, I don't need to learn to play the piano." "My health is fantastic. Certainly I'm better off than half of the 'health-nut' joggers in the world." "I can be more comfortable watching television than going out with her."

"Sour-grapes" and "sweet-lemon" thinking are examples of rationalization. Rationalization, in a psychological sense, is the process of thinking up logical, socially approved reasons to justify certain behaviors and beliefs, or to soften the disappointment of not reaching goals. Through rationalization it becomes easy to justify the absolute necessity of buying an expensive new car, or of going out with a friend rather than studying. At its extreme, individuals can even justify and explain away murder as being noble and necessary. Less extreme antisocial behavior can also be justified, such as, "Why pay taxes? The money will be squandered by the government anyway," or, "Why be honest about it? No one else is."

Rationalization Isn't All Bad

Rationalization can also be defined as the process of making something conform to reason, making sense out of it, or explaining something on rational grounds. Defined this way, rationalization is a healthy endeavor, something we do continually as a necessary part of problem solving and decision making. If something doesn't work, we look for logical explanations as to why it doesn't. If we have made mistakes we need to uncover rational explanations for why we did so, in order to avoid making the same errors in the future. When making decisions, we attempt to reach rational, objective conclusions about various options.

Even though these behaviors technically involve a rationalization process, each of these mental actions is a necessary aspect of healthy living. Rationalization is also helpful as a defense mechanism when we fail. If we find goals that we have set for ourselves to be truly unattainable, it makes good sense to remind ourselves that we can be happy anyway. We need also to keep the option open of forsaking goals that we find are unworthy of the time and effort needed to reach them.

In short, rationalization can be both a good and a bad thing, depending on how it is defined and utilized. On one hand, it is a process that can help us make reasonable decisions, and it can help us live comfortably with negative circumstances beyond our control. On the other hand, rationalization may amount to self-deception. It may make us less able to learn from our mistakes and more likely to maintain false beliefs or delusions. It may cause us to give up important goals prematurely, or we may use it to justify actions that hurt ourselves or others.

The Thin Line Between Rationalizing and Thinking Rationally

In order to avoid confusion, rationalization in its negative sense will be labeled *rationalizing* from here on, and rationalization in its positive sense will be identified as *thinking rationally*. Obviously, there is a thin line between the two. Where does an objective consideration of the facts (thinking rationally) leave off and rationalization begin? There are at least four clues that may help you identify when you have slipped into rationalizing.

Do I Become Upset When My Reasons Are Questioned?

If you become upset when your reasoning is questioned, self-deception could be involved. You may be operating on assumptions that basically don't make sense to you, and underlying guilt feelings and insecurity may lead to defensiveness and excessive emotion when your reasoning is questioned.

For example, Kevin had a long history of sexual involvement with women outside of marriage. He joined the Church and amended his ways—at least for a while. He soon found himself, however, slipping back into old behavior patterns. About the same time, his attitude toward the Church changed. He began to think that the Church was overly strict, that it was led by "a bunch of old men who are not in touch with reality," and that, in general, the gospel as taught by the Church was not true. This way of thinking was essentially a "sour-grapes" rationalization process used by Kevin to counter his guilt about behavior that obviously contradicted his belief system.

Evidence for the fact that Kevin's loss of testimony was due to rationalization and not to thinking rationally came, in part, from his tendency to get very upset when his thinking was challenged. He would get defensive and critical of the Church whenever the issues involved came into focus. He could not discuss the Church without experiencing unproductive emotion, and he actively tried to market his negative opinions about the Church to others. His emotional response, defensiveness, and critical comments all were suggestive that he was not honest with himself with respect to his beliefs. (Keep in mind that many people show no emotion on the surface but do get upset privately when their thinking is challenged. This also is a clue that rationalization is involved.)

On the other hand, Mary joined the Church very much against the wishes of her parents and extended family. When she was questioned about her faith, she felt somewhat embarrassed, but she was not exceptionally defensive and she made no attempt to tear down the faith of other family members. She had made a rational choice. She knew it. She knew that God knew it, and she made no apology for her new faith. Mary's lack of emotional upset was evidence that her conversion resulted from a process of rational thinking, not rationalizing.

Now obviously, whether someone gets upset or not when his thinking is questioned is not always an indication that rationalization has occurred. We are often annoyed when someone attacks our thinking. Most everyone gets upset to some extent when he is criticized for what he believes, especially when he values the opinion of the criticizer. But the question, "Do I get upset when my reasoning is questioned?" is still relevant as a possible indicator of rationalization. The upset may indicate underlying guilt that is being masked by a rationalization process.

Do I Avoid Obvious Contradictions to My Views?

Another possible indicator of rationalization is a refusal to hear counterarguments or a tendency to avoid recognizing obvious contradictions to the logic of one's position. Some smokers, for example, avoid reading about medical discoveries on the effects of smoking, and they stay away from discussions of the subject whenever possible. They may also argue with the data and with claims of the medical community even though the facts are well established. This provides evidence that their support of smoking is a result of rationalizing, not a result of rational thinking.

Does My Belief Contradict Gospel Principles?

Another means of checking out whether you are thinking rationally or not is provided by comparing your views to gospel principles. This point was made centuries ago by the prophet Mormon, who suggested that if our thinking is correct, it will move us to do good.

> For behold, the Spirit of Christ is given to every man, that he may know good from evil; wherefore, I show unto you the way to judge; for every thing which inviteth to do good, and to persuade to believe in Christ, is sent forth by the power and gift of Christ; wherefore ye may know with a perfect knowledge it is of God. (Moroni 7:16.)

A third point to remember, then, is that if we find ourselves moving away from gospel principles, such as honesty, faith, chastity, or service, or moving away from doing good, we are probably rationalizing.

What Is the General Consequence of My Belief?

Expanding on this idea somewhat, we can often identify rationalization by evaluating the consequences of certain behaviors in our lives. Jerry, for example, was an introvert. He often thought about asking a girl for a date, or about becoming more socially active in other ways, but he would usually decide against it. His thought pattern was something like the following:

"Nobody will want to go out with me. I will just make a fool out of myself. I don't have what it takes socially. I'm better off staying home. Why force myself to do something I don't want to? I don't need anyone else. I can be happier single."

Unfortunately, his decision to avoid social contact and the rationalization process that supported his decision led to a very uncomfortable life. Jerry told himself that he was happy and that he didn't need others, but in reality he was very unhappy. Jerry was negative, critical, easily annoyed, and he found little fun or excitement in living. The fact that he was unhappy and relatively unproductive was a clue to Jerry that he was kidding himself. Once he became aware of his rationalization, he gained the motivation necessary to improve his situation.

Jerry's experience suggests that, in order to uncover rationalization, we might ask ourselves, "Does what I am telling myself help me reach my goals? Does it help me feel the way I want to feel?" A no to either or both questions almost guarantees that we are not thinking rationally about the issue.

Four Criteria of Rationalization

In summary, then, four criteria that suggest rationalization are:
1. Do I get upset when my thinking is challenged?
2. Do I avoid counterarguments or resist well-documented evidence?
3. Does the way I think about it move me from gospel principles or good works?
4. Does the way I think about it keep me from feeling the way I want to feel, or does it keep me from doing what I want to do?

Julie applied these criteria and decided she had a problem with her thinking. Early in her life, Julie came to the conclusion that she was a person of little worth. She falsely assumed that she had little to offer others and that the world would be better off without her. In the process of therapy she fought hard to maintain her conviction of her lack of worth. She decided that compliments and support from others were contrived, and she assumed that it was a gross rationalization of the facts to assume that she was actually a talented, worthwhile human being.

According to the criteria of rationality suggested above, Julie's belief that she had little worth was a rationalization. Julie became emotional when her conclusions about herself were questioned. She avoided counterarguments, and she refused to accept the evidence of her worth as clearly stated in the scriptures and elsewhere. Her thinking about herself eventually contributed to immorality and a lack of effort to serve others. Her assumptions about her worth caused her to feel bad and inhibited her progress toward her goals. She was not thinking rationally, as determined by all four criteria listed above.

Actually, it is not necessary that all four criteria be satisfied in order to conclude that rationalization is occurring. We may be kidding ourselves when even one of the criteria applies. It should also be noted that, as Julie's case indicates, we can rationalize in a negative as well as in a positive direction. It is often thought that rationalization is the process of avoiding the truth in order to build ourselves up. However, we also distort reality when we unjustifiably tear ourselves down.

Common Rationalizations to Look For

Rationalizations usually lose their power to affect behavior once they are recognized and understood for what they are. Kidding ourselves doesn't do much good if we understand that we are kidding ourselves. Several common rationalizations are suggested below under various headings, along with countering logic for each one. Before moving on, however, we need to emphasize an important point. Everything in this chapter is designed to help you check *your* thinking for rationalizations. It should be apparent that pointing their rationalizations out to others, at least in situations in which your advice has not been sought, will normally block further communication and promote hostility.

Common Emotional-Control Rationalizations

Several common rationalizations used to justify unhealthy emotion are identified below, along with ideas that refute each one. These rationalizations can get in the way of developing emotional control, a primary but difficult goal for us all.

Other people or events make me upset. This point was addressed in chapter 6. People and events influence our thinking and subsequently our emotions, but others cannot control our feelings or thought processes. Suppose that I want to lose weight, but without thinking about it my wife buys a dozen doughnuts. She inadvertently leaves several doughnuts on the kitchen counter, and I can't resist the temptation to eat them. I could blame my wife for the fact that I ate the doughnuts, but that doesn't seem fair. After all, she didn't tie me to a chair and force-feed me. It is true that I would not have eaten the doughnuts if they had not been there. It is also true that my wife might have been more thoughtful and either not purchased them in the first place or kept them out of sight. But I can't blame her for the fact that *I* made the decision to eat them.

Suppose that my wife says something unkind, and I get upset about it. True, I would not have become angry if the comment had not been made, and my wife probably should not have said the unkind thing. Yet, in the final analysis, I am the one responsible for how I react to the comment. On a good day I might pass it off, and on another day I might not.

It makes sense for us to protect ourselves from negative situations when possible, and it is certainly appropriate to ask for the cooperation of others. Still, we must accept final responsibility for how we feel, in the same sense that I had to accept final responsibility for eating the doughnuts. Other people or events don't make us upset; we do that to ourselves.

It isn't possible to control my emotions. Normally, the assumption that emotional control is not possible is pure rationalization. Everyone has bad moments, but all of us can learn to manage our feelings. The fact that we don't always do so doesn't mean that we cannot; it just means that we haven't learned how yet. Ideas on how to control emotions were given in chapter 6.

Of course there are rare situations in which emotional control is very difficult, as in cases involving problems in body chemistry or stress overload. For instance, someone who is severely depressed may find himself locked into a pattern of emotional responses that are very difficult to control. But even where circumstances make emotional control difficult or temporarily impossible, those circumstances can normally be changed over time. Someone unable to handle situations emotionally can go to a professional for help in sorting out his problems and finding solutions.

It's just the way I am. Obviously, emotional experience is a healthy aspect of living. Emotional monotones are not much fun to be around, and they are normally not very happy. They do avoid negative emotions, but only at the expense of positive ones. On the other hand, some people get so emotional about various issues that they are also hard to live with, and are quite unhappy people.

Unemotional people will often rationalize their positions by pointing out how much better they behave than people who are more emotional. They may say, "Look how strong I am." But they overlook the fact that it often takes more courage and humility to allow oneself to feel and show emotion. Emotional insulation protects a person from some of the negative elements of life; unfortunately, it also prevents him from feeling many sweet elements of life.

On the other end of the continuum, those whose emotions are out of control will often say that they are just being "up front," open, and honest with feelings. "You don't have to wonder where I'm coming from," they say. But in these cases, "honest" communication of feelings is sometimes a facade for negative and manipulative interaction and an excuse to vent out-of-control feelings.

Whether someone is overly emotional or not emotional enough, it should be recognized that he has *learned* to operate that way. In my opinion, it is incorrect to say that a person is born very emotional or very unemotional and that he cannot change. Emotional response patterns can be changed if we have the incentive to do so and an understanding of how to proceed.

Common Behavior-Control Rationalizations

We often excuse our bad habits through rationalization. Examples of how people commonly do so, and logic that contradicts the rationalization process, are given below.

My bad habit hurts no one but me. Some rationalize their failure to control bad habits on the grounds that they hurt only themselves, or that control would cause problems for others. "If I didn't sleep in, I would be terrible to live with." "If I couldn't have my morning coffee, watch out." In this kind of thinking, the bad habit almost becomes a virtue because of the protection it seemingly affords others.

The problem with such thinking is that it helps lock an individual in an unhealthy behavior pattern. Then, too, others typically *do* suffer, even when the bad habits involved are personal in nature. Bad habits that affect spirituality or Church standing hurt the doer the most, but they also rob those close to him of the strength and power that might otherwise come through him to them.

In a world in which we are interdependent, and in which relationships are so important, we have virtually no personal problems that do not, at least indirectly, have an impact on others.

What I do (or don't do) isn't so bad. Why worry about it? Of course, it is a common human tendency to make big issues out of small things. We do tend to "awfulize" and to get very concerned about relatively unimportant things. As indicated in chapter 3, one of the worst things we can do is to get overconcerned about self-improvement. Becoming too intense actually makes developing personal power more difficult. Furthermore, worry is always wasted effort. We need to either do something about the situation or decide not to worry.

Even so, the truth is that bad habits have a cost associated with them. We need to be supportive of ourselves, and to not take our problems too seriously, but we must also not kid ourselves into assuming that a bad habit is not so bad after all. If you wonder about whether or not a specific bad habit needs to be eliminated, refer again to the criteria of rationalization given earlier. If the habit makes it difficult for you to feel the way you want to, if it is an obstacle to your goals, or if it contradicts gospel principles, don't accept it as being natural, normal behavior.

At the same time, keep in mind the need to be moderate in self-improvement effort. Don't attempt to eliminate all bad habits at once. It is not necessary to run faster or labor more than your ability allows (see D&C 10:4).

I'm too old; I'm not smart enough; I don't have what it takes. Unfortunately, many people undermine their faith in themselves by constantly finding excuses for failure *before* they have failed. If you have given a goal your best effort but have been unsuccessful, it makes sense to consider the factors involved. You may be too short to play professional basketball, or too old to be accepted into medical school. You may not have the intellectual power or manual dexterity to be a neurosurgeon. But you shouldn't count yourself out before you have given worthwhile goals a try. Typically, we underestimate our abilities and overestimate the abilities of those who have achieved success. Normally, the only difference between them and us is a combination of the faith they have in their ability, and large amounts of practice and experience. Usually there *is* a way to achieve personal goals.

Of course, the only eternally critical goal we have—living a Christlike life—is attainable by all of us. Everyone can develop charity, humility, honesty, chastity, patience, and the other personal attributes associated with celestial personalities. No one is too old, too retarded, or too handicapped to develop a Christlike personality. The temple teaches this lesson well. The same promises are given to the less intellectually endowed and to the genius alike. In the temple, the rich and the poor, great and small, beautiful and not so beautiful are all uniformly blessed.

Worthwhile social goals are likewise open to all. We may assume that we are not smart enough to get along with him or that we are not attractive enough to be accepted by her. But actually, there are only four important criteria that I can think of for being accepted by others. (1) You need to have self-confidence, or a conviction that you are an important person (whether the world defines you as such or not). (2) You need to care for others enough to be relatively tolerant of their imperfections. (3) You need to be involved in helping and supporting others. (4) You need to spend time with others. Wit, charm, good looks, and money may or may not be helpful, but these attributes are *not* necessary. We are socially limited only when we *assume* that we are handicapped in some way. (Obviously, however, even if the four criteria listed above are in place on your side of the relationship, there are some people with whom you will not be able to relate comfortably because of *their* problems.)

In summary, make sure that if you are going to find reasons for failing to reach a goal, you do it after dedicated effort, rather than before. Don't give up prematurely by selling yourself short. Also remember that there are ultimately no justifiable reasons for failing to develop Christlike attributes. That is where we need to concentrate our self-development efforts. Likewise, there are no justifiable reasons for counting ourselves out socially. We all have unlimited amounts of love to give self and others, and that is all that really counts in developing meaningful relationships.

Common Rationalizations for Not Reaching Out Socially

Many people inhibit their social experience through rationalizations like those identified below. Counterlogic is again presented that contradicts each rationalization.

It is more comfortable to stay home. Social goals are often difficult to reach because a socially withdrawn person usually is more comfortable staying home than he is going out. Of course, an individual who avoids social contact is more comfortable at home only in the short run. In the longer term, social isolation frequently breeds depression, self-hate, boredom, and reduced productivity.

This classic dichotomy between short-term comfort and long-term interests can be relieved somewhat by following suggestions given earlier, such as building self-esteem, changing your think-ing, and self-reinforcement. Even so, at some point, an individual wanting to be more socially outgoing must "bite the bullet" and put himself into social situations, whether he is uncomfortable doing so or not. Practice is needed, and nothing short of actual interaction with others will suffice.

I will just be hurt if I reach out. This "Why bother?" rationali-zation is common in many areas of our lives. Obviously, a person loses motivation whenever he develops a defeatist attitude re-garding some effort that he might undertake. This fear is often based in actual rejection. Socially withdrawn individuals often have been rejected by others, or, at least, they are more likely to be rejected. Shyness itself results in holding back from others (often making the person seem proud or "stuck up"), and it can lead to ineffective social responses that turn off the interest others might have in a relationship.

Furthermore, those who are socially insecure are generally open to relationships primarily with two kinds of people. The first are "gate crashers." These are insensitive, self-centered, selfish individuals who come crashing through a shy person's defenses. Gate crashers are either too insensitive to notice barriers to social contact or too selfishly motivated to care. The second group of likely relationship candidates are those with obvious problems. This group is attractive to the shy person because he usually thinks, "Here is someone who won't reject me because he has so many problems (so much need) himself." Actually, the probability of being hurt by either "gate crashers" or individuals with obvious personal problems is exceptionally high. Unfortunately, the insecure individual doesn't often invite in those who are levelheaded and potentially good prospects for stable relationships.

As suggested above, at some point the insecure individual must "bite the bullet" and risk rejection. Frank is socially in-secure, but he is also a very good baseball player. I asked him if he ever worried about striking out at the plate. Predictably, his response was, "Certainly!" I then asked him how he felt when he struck out. "Terrible!" Next I asked how he felt when he hit a home run. Frank then related one of the most exciting moments in his life when he won the game for his team with an extra-inning home run. What if Frank had been so afraid of striking out that he had not gone up to bat that day? We can save ourselves from failure if we don't participate in life, but we also sacrifice the possibility of success.

Not all relationships will work out, but then no relationship is possible without some effort and some risk. The person who stays away from social contact out of fear of rejection ironically experiences rejection—the very thing he is trying so hard to avoid.

I won't have anything to say. Concern about not being an effective conversationalist is another common excuse for failure to reach out to people. Usually conversational problems are not based on an absence of something to talk about, but rather on excess concern about saying the "right thing." Insecure individuals will often carefully filter potential comments silently before making them aloud. The intent is to guarantee that the comment is appropriate, won't be embarrassing, will "make points," won't hurt anyone else's feelings, and so forth. Unfortunately, the result of this mental screening process is a somewhat mechanical conversation style, not much to say at all, and missed conversational opportunities. Someone who carefully screens all comments before making them usually finds that by the time he has judged a remark to be appropriate, the opportunity to share it has passed.

Normally, the single most important thing that you can do to improve your conversational ability is to decide not to worry about filtering each comment for appropriateness. Just say it! It also helps to remember the value of asking questions. People are rarely offended when you ask questions designed to help you get to know them better. Current-event questions (e.g., did you see that . . . , or, did you hear about . . . ?) are also generally appropriate.

Feeling uncomfortable about your ability to converse with others is reason to further develop your conversational skill, not justification to avoid people. Conversational ability is like any other skill. It can be developed, but it takes practice.

Watch Your Rationalizing, but Not Too Closely

Only a few of the hundreds of rationalizations common among us have been identified in this chapter. But these examples should be sufficient to illustrate two concepts: (1) We can usually determine whether or not we are rationalizing by applying the four criteria described above, and (2) Seeing through to the faulty logic of rationalizations will dilute their negative influence. As a concluding comment on this subject, however, a cautionary note needs to be added.

Even though this chapter is recommending that we analyze our thinking, there is always the danger of our being overly analytical with ourselves. Carol wants to know whether or not she should marry Richard. She has prayed long and hard about it and, after periods of prayer, always feels positive about proceeding. Going ahead with the marriage also seems right since Richard generally satisfies the list of characteristics that Carol wants in a mate. Carol also feels comfortable when she is with Richard, and her parents are strongly supportive of her marrying Richard.

Unfortunately, Carol has analyzed the situation to death. She gets so caught up in thinking, "What if this were to happen?" or "What if that were to happen?" and so involved in second-guessing herself that she can't reach a decision once and for all. "Richard seems right, but what if I am just rationalizing in order to avoid the embarrassment of calling off the engagement? What if I am feeling positive only because I haven't the courage to do what I really feel I should do?" Actually, Carol's main problem is that she is a perfectionist. She is waiting for a time in which she has perfect faith or perfect knowledge in her decision to marry Richard. Of course, perfect knowledge, regarding most of life's decisions, is rare.

Certainly the decision about whom to marry is an important one, and it deserves prayer and careful consideration. But second-guessing yourself and being overly analytical can obstruct your progress toward goals as effectively as can too little analysis.

The fact is, that if we look long and hard enough, we can almost always find reasons to assume that we are rationalizing. Rationalization can become a catchall term that is made to apply to most any situation. Since no one is perfect, a person can always do better. Since we all have many responsibilities, we cannot give a hundred percent of our effort all of the time, nor can we do our absolute best with respect to any one particular responsibility. Since we generally can't predict the future with absolute precision, we cannot be entirely sure of many of the decisions we make. We often have to choose between mutually exclusive things that both ought to be done, and we can't always do everything we ought to. For these and other reasons, there is always room for us to doubt our thinking and to assume that we are rationalizing.

Balance Is the Key

As in many things, balance is a key principle here. We need to become aware of the times that we are kidding ourselves. At the same time, being self-critical or spending too much time in self-analysis will be counterproductive. If you wonder where you are on the continuum, between too little and too much self-analysis, look for clues in how your life is progressing. If you find immobilization, lack of productivity, or difficulty controlling emotions, these are clues that you might be temporarily stuck at one extreme or the other.

Chapter 9

Putting It All Together

Each of the preceding chapters has emphasized an element useful in increasing personal power. Of course, you can bring together ideas from all the chapters when you are developing a plan for overcoming specific self-direction problems. Examples of how you might do this can be found in subsequent sections of this chapter for selected problems, such as low self-esteem, critical treatment of others, shyness, procrastination, hot temper, and unwanted sexual behavior.

Keep in mind that the illustrations that follow are examples only, and the exact strategies described might not be relevant in your situation. It should also be noted that the remainder of this chapter is not intended for the general reader so much as it is for the person facing one or more of the specific problems identified.

Ideas to Help Build Faith in Yourself

Self-confidence is an *essential* ingredient in developing personal power. With it, our efforts flow smoothly and almost easily; without it, we are immobilized and find self-direction very difficult. Take a few minutes to assess whether or not you need to improve with respect to the factors listed below that affect self-confidence. If you or someone you care about needs to make improvement, one or two suggestions that can help are identified under each issue.

1. Am I truly converted to an understanding of the eternal worth of my spirit?
   —Search the scriptures for references to the eternal worth of man.
   —Write down all the reasons you can think of that support the conclusion that you have an infinite worth and potential.
   —Pray for a conviction of your worth and value.
2. Do I keep separate in my mind the worth of what I do and the worth of what I am?
   —When you notice that you have done something stupid, remind yourself, "But I know that I am *not* stupid. Brilliant people regularly do stupid things."
   —When you have failed, remind yourself that you have failed to do a *particular* thing at a *particular* moment. It doesn't mean that you have failed at life, or even that you will continue to fail at the particular thing.
   —When you are upset with yourself, think of the small child who does unproductive, immature things, yet who obviously has an infinite worth. We are all little children in some sense.
3. Are my standards for myself reasonable? (Standards are normally too high if you frequently feel like a failure, if you feel great pressure to produce, or if you cannot relax easily.)
   —Plan a little time for yourself every day.
   —Make sure you are balanced in your response to service requests or to favors asked of you. For most people that means not always saying yes, but also, not always saying no.
   —Frequently remind yourself that you are doing the best that you can under the circumstances, and *that is good enough.*
   —In your interpersonal relationships, emphasize charity, love, and patience over performance, tasks, and things.

4. Am I too self-critical?
   —Monitor self-critical comments for some period of time. (See chapter 6.)
   —Say "stop" whenever you become aware of a self-criticism.
   —Frequently remind yourself that you are doing the best that you can under the circumstances, and *that is good enough.*
5. Do I recognize my accomplishments and think good things about myself?
   —List all of your positive attributes and the good things you do. Have someone you trust review your list and add to it.
   —Make a serious effort to say "thanks" to yourself for relatively minor accomplishments as well as for big successes.
   —Write down at the end of the day all the things you feel good about (even a little bit) that happened during the day.
   —Say something positive about yourself whenever you look in a mirror, or when entering a room in a social situation. Examples: "My hair looks nice." "I'm an intelligent person." "I have nothing to fear but fear itself."
6. Do I act as if I am a person of worth and value?
   —Make a goal to smile more, look people in the eye, have a firm handshake, walk upright and confidently.
   —Remind yourself regularly in uncomfortable settings that you are just like everyone else there. All are children of God. Everyone is of equal worth.
   —Remember that success depends on love, confidence, respect, and other variables equally available to all. Beauty, wit, charm, money, and position may be nice but are *not* necessary.
7. Am I actively involved in good causes?
   —Write notes of thanks to others. Be complimentary of others.
   —Pick a secret friend and anonymously do a series of nice things for that person.
   —Get physically active in some way (sports, exercising, walking).
   —Actively associate yourself with groups or organizations that are doing things that you feel are appropriate and worthwhile.

8. Do I usually set moderate (as opposed to high-risk or low-risk) goals?

—As you establish goals, regularly ask yourself what the realistic chances are of success. If the chance of success is either very high or very low, consider changing the goal to something of more moderate risk.

Again, self-confidence is a base from which personal power can develop. If lack of self-confidence is a problem for you, reread chapter 3. Then begin activities such as those suggested above that can help you to develop more faith in yourself.

A Plan to Become Less Critical

Points to Remember

Don't become too concerned about reaching this goal immediately. Becoming overly intense will normally result in more, rather than less, self-criticism. Remember also that it defeats your purpose to be self-critical whenever you catch yourself being critical. ("You dummy! Why are you always critical!") A final point to remember is that to reduce criticism you must have faith that people do their best when given support, not criticism. (This issue was discussed in chapter 3.)

Step 1: Define and Research the Problem

Before you work on the problem, you must define criticism precisely enough so that you will be aware of when it is and is not occurring. Make a list of examples of critical responses (both verbal and nonverbal thoughts and actions) that you are going to attempt to avoid. It may be useful to then ask someone you trust to review your list for clarity and completeness.

Next, try to identify some of the root issues causing your overly critical behavior. This can usually be accomplished by a series of "why" questions: "Why am I critical?" "Why do I react the way I do?" "Why does that bother me?" After you have answered one "why" question, ask another about your answer, in a repetitive fashion, looking for even more basic issues. (Why am I critical of Hank? Because I can't tolerate his behavior. Why can't I tolerate his behavior? Because it is embarrassing. Why is it embarrassing? and so forth.)

Next, establish a system for recording incidents of criticism over a one- to two-week period. This can be done simply as follows:

	Self	Husband	Julie	David	Others
Day 1					
Day 2					

Try to determine when you tend to be most critical, what form your criticism usually takes, factors related to being critical, and so forth.

Step 2: Develop a Strategy for Solving the Problem

Based on the information obtained in step 1, develop a strategy for solving the problem. Although your plan should be personalized, it may be patterned after the following plan. (This plan involved a homemaker with three small children.)

Modify my external environment

1. Sign up for aerobic dancing (twice a week).
2. Arrange for a babysitter for one afternoon each week.
3. Arrange with the family for a cook's night off once or twice a week.
4. Put notes around the house, such as "peace," "calm," to remind me of my goal.

Modify my internal environment

1. Every time something negative happens, I will repeat several times in my mind:
   —It's not that important.
   —It's not worth getting upset about.
   —The best way to get cooperation is to be supportive and nonjudgmental.
   —How can I solve the problem without anger?
2. Repeat in my mind (out loud if alone) several times a day:
   —I can be less critical and everyone, including me, will produce even more.

—I am a person of infinite worth and value.

—Life will be so much more comfortable when I reach my goal.

Reinforcement plan

1. Keep a record of critical comments (same format as in step 1).

2. For every three-hour block of time that I am not critical of anyone, I will devote at least half an hour to a favorite activity:

   —walk

   —good book

   —relax with good music

3. For every day I don't criticize I will give myself points toward a weekend away with my husband. (Seven days without criticism = one weekend away.)

Spiritual plan

1. Spend a few minutes in quiet reflection after daily prayers.

2. Pray specifically for positive thoughts and feelings of love to replace negative, critical thinking.

Step 3: Evaluate the Results

Based on the record of critical comments you have maintained as part of the reinforcement plan, determine your level of success in reaching your goal. Where more improvement is desired, change the techniques utilized in the plan somewhat and repeat the process.

A Plan for Becoming More Socially Outgoing

Since becoming more outgoing and extroverted depends a great deal on self-confidence, begin work in this area by carefully reviewing the factors related to self-esteem listed at the beginning of this chapter. Steps in developing self-confidence should be taken prior to, or in conjunction with, direct efforts to become more outgoing.

As with other self-development issues, pushing too hard will reduce the chances of success. You may need to press yourself initially to put yourself in social situations, but once you are there, your strategy should emphasize methods for developing relaxed, natural feelings and behavior.

Remember also to analyze the rationalizations you use in support of not being involved socially to the extent that you would like. Three common ones were reviewed earlier. Other rationalizations will come to mind as you follow the research ideas outlined below.

Step 1: Define and Research the Problem

1. List all of your friends by name on paper. (Include relatives that you consider to be friends.)
   — Put an asterisk by the names of the friends with whom you can openly share feelings.
   — Record daily for one month the amount of time you spend interacting informally with each friend on your list. Add names where necessary.
   — Underline the names of friends that you would like to get to know better.
2. Whenever you are debating whether or not to participate in a social experience, *write down* (don't do it in your head) the thoughts that come to mind as you make the decision such as:

Pro	Con
I should go.	I won't know what to say.
I have to meet people.	I'll be bored.

3. Ask yourself a series of "why" questions regarding why it is hard for you to be outgoing.

Step 2: Develop a Strategy for Solving the Problem

The following plan was developed for a twenty-eight-year-old bachelor based on the results of the research steps suggested above.

Change the external environment
1. Buy a nice outfit or two; get my hair styled.
2. Place self-confidence notes to myself around the apartment. ("You have a lot to offer." "You are equal in value to anyone.")
3. If I get anxious in a social situation, I will go to the bathroom or some other place temporarily, rethink the situation, and return to the group.

Change the internal environment
1. Repeat in my mind (out loud when alone) the following thoughts several times a day:
   —Acceptance and love are what count. I have as much of those to give as anyone.
   —I don't have to prove anything to anyone.
   —I just need to care. I don't have to be witty or profound.
   —I will be rejected and alone if I don't risk. I have nothing to lose by reaching out.
   —I don't have to always hit a home run. I can just practice batting.
   —There is no one perfect time or perfect way in which to interact with someone else.
2. I will relax. I will picture myself having natural, comfortable social exchanges in different settings. (A procedure for doing so can be found in chapter 9 of *The Art of Effective Living*.) Practice mentally in this manner for ten to fifteen minutes twice a day. Imagine the scenes in specific detail (what people are wearing, facial expressions, sounds, smells, what is said, and so forth).

Reinforcement plan
1. Make a favorite activity (reading newspaper, having dinner) contingent on making a somewhat difficult social contact daily. Choose from the following list:
   —Call someone to say thank you or to congratulate him for something.
   —Invite someone I don't know very well to share an activity.

—Ask for a favor or offer help to a friend.

—Ask a question of someone I don't know well.

—Start up a conversation with a stranger.

—Ask directions from a stranger (even if I know the way).

—Share personal information with a friend.

2. Give my self points toward permission to purchase a new stereo system based on time with friends and a 50 percent increase in interaction time with friends over a one-month period. (Note: Repeating the first suggestion under step 1 on a monthly basis will indicate time spent with people and new friends made.)

Spiritual plan

1. Complete a scripture search for indications of (a) my worth in the eternal scheme of things, and (b) the importance of the family and interpersonal relationships.

2. Pray for faith in myself and for faith in what I have to offer others.

Step 3: Evaluate the Results

Based on monthly assessments, determine the level of progress made and make changes in procedures where necessary.

A Plan for Overcoming Procrastination

Points to Remember

As suggested earlier, all self-development strategies need to be personalized. What works for one person may not work for another. What works at one time may not work later. Since causes of procrastination are highly individualized, the need to personalize is especially important when the issue is overcoming procrastination. Causes of procrastination vary, of course, from person to person, but they also vary from issue to issue. The specific kinds of things typically procrastinated need to be understood, along with the general characteristics of the tendency itself.

Rationalizations are involved in procrastination to a larger extent than they are in some other self-development areas. Keep in mind the need to understand what kind of thinking supports procrastination and the need to move toward more productive conceptualizations.

Step 1: Define and Research the Problem

1. Follow the plan given in chapter 5 by completing a daily record of activities over a one- to two-week period.
2. When faced with decisions about whether or not to work on specific projects, note *on paper* (not in your head) what you are thinking:
   —I haven't time now.
   —It's too big a hassle to get out materials.
   —Nobody cares about it anyway.
3. Ask yourself why the thoughts written down under point 2 above bother you. Normally, additional issues will then come to mind:
   —I don't want to start if I can't finish.
   —If I get going I won't be able to stop.
   —The kids never do anything for me.

Step 2: Develop a Strategy for Solving the Problem

The plan given below was completed for a young mother of two who is a single head of household with a career.

Modify my external environment

1. Gather materials for a project together and leave them out. (As incentive and a reminder to get the project completed.)
2. Replace television with radio as background for work projects at home.
3. Unplug the telephone Tuesday, Wednesday, and Thursday evenings until nine-thirty. (Inform friends and relatives.)
4. Change work assignments, giving more responsibility to the kids.

Modify my internal environment

1. Repeat the following ideas several times a day:

—I don't have to complete everything I start right away; I can at least get started.

—Many things are worth doing whether they are done perfectly or not.

—I am operating at full capacity. I don't have to feel guilty when I turn down requests to take on more responsibility.

—I am doing the best I can under the circumstances, and that is good enough.

—Important calls will come through later. I don't have to be available all the time.

2. When at home, I will remember to drop my shoulders a little, move a little more slowly, and practice deep breathing occasionally while repeating the word "relax."

Reinforcement plan

1. On Sunday, identify one long-delayed project that can be realistically completed during the week. Write the project on the calendar. Give myself half an hour of a pleasant activity (book, TV) for every hour I work on the project.

2. Where possible, make the negative aspects of projects more positive by combining them with good music, working with the children or a friend, generating pleasant thoughts while working on the project, and so forth.

Spiritual plan

1. Listen for a few minutes after daily prayers.

2. Turn more things over to the Lord rather than worry about them.

Step 3: Evaluate the Results

Note the number of projects completed and the general feelings of productivity you have. You might also want to repeat the daily log exercise under step 1. Comparing your first and second recordings should indicate the improvements that have been made. Where more progress is desired, modify procedures somewhat and repeat the steps outlined above.

A Plan for Temper Control

Points to Remember

Controlling one's temper takes effort, but the goal should not be all consuming. As suggested earlier, focusing too intently often increases frustration, which actually may increase anger. It should also be remembered that temper control essentially means thought control. Controlling anger after it has developed is much more difficult than not letting it develop in the first place.

In this regard, the fact is often pointed out that it is damaging to keep anger inside. But on the other hand, it usually doesn't do much good to vent negative feelings. Doing so often leads to guilt, and angry outbursts often damage interpersonal relationships. The only genuinely effective solution lies in thinking in such a way that anger seldom develops at all. Of course, this is much easier to do if self-confidence is strong. Refer again to the notes on self-esteem at the beginning of this chapter.

Step 1: Define and Research the Problem

1. Devise an "anger scale" in your mind with one being not angry at all and ten being almost to the point of blind rage. Occasionally (eight or nine times on a random basis) throughout the day, pick a number between one and ten that represents your level of anger at the moment. Record the time, level of anger, and general circumstances at the time of recording over a one-week period.
2. Each time that anger develops to the point that it is noticeable, record information under the following headings:

    Time   *Situation*   *Thoughts About Situation*

Step 2: Develop a Strategy for Solving the Problem

The plan described here applies to a twenty-nine-year-old man who is married and has four small children.

Change my external environment

1. Send the kids to their room when discipline is required, instead of intervening verbally or physically.
2. Stop for fifteen minutes at a nearby park before arriving home. Concentrate on total body relaxation and pleasant thoughts during this time.
3. Get a duplicate set of common tools for the family, and lock my tools up, keeping the only key.

Change my internal environment

1. Repeat the following thoughts in my mind several times a day:
   —It really doesn't matter. Nothing is worth getting upset about.
   —I refuse to make myself a double victim.
   —I won't let anyone or anything control my feelings.
   —I get more of what I want with honey than with vinegar.
2. When my anger level rises, remove myself temporarily and concentrate on relaxing my body and putting myself mentally in a very pleasant situation (beach, forest, etc.).

Reinforcement strategy

1. When angry, do as many pushups as possible while at the same time thinking every angry thought possible about the situation, followed by relaxing and thinking again the thoughts under "Changing my internal environment" above.
2. During periods of high stress (evenings and weekends at home), give myself permission to enjoy a favorite activity for half an hour for every one-and-one-half hours without an angry reaction.

Spiritual plan

1. Pray for help specifically to be patient of others' imperfections and for love to replace anger.
2. Ask myself what the Lord would *think* in this situation, as well as what he would do.

Step 3: Evaluate the Results

Based on the record kept of angry feelings and outbursts, evaluate the success of the behavior change program. Make modifications in the plan where necessary until the goal is achieved.

A Plan to Control Unwanted Sexual Activity

Points to Remember

The more one thinks about sexual activity, whether in terms of how wrong it is or how enjoyable, the higher the likelihood that it will occur. Thinking about it in any form will often build desire.

It helps to remember that frustration, especially involving feelings of low self-esteem, increases the desire for sexual intimacy. It is therefore important that a person not condemn himself severely because of past sexual problems. (Condemning the *practice* is different.) It is also important to keep a generally positive outlook when possible, and to avoid circumstances that result in high stress or frustration. Refer again to the ideas about building self-confidence at the beginning of the chapter.

Step 1: Define and Research the Problem

1. Analyze past experience and *write down* answers to the following questions:
   —Where does it happen?
   —When is it most likely to happen?
   —What leads up to it?
   —What do I do afterward?
   —When does it never happen?
2. Identify factors in the environment that create sexual interest.

Step 2: Develop a Strategy for Solving the Problem

The following plan was devised by a twenty-one-year-old male who lives alone and who desires to avoid sexual activity prior to marriage.

Modify my external environment

1. Avoid movies rated "R" and "X."
2. Spend more time with friends; more physical activity; more fun.
3. Avoid bringing dates to my apartment.
4. Place pictures of temples in my apartment and car (rotate the pictures regularly).

Modify my internal environment

1. Emphasize self-compliments and repeat self-building thoughts several times a day:
   —I am a person of infinite worth and value.
   —The Lord has a great work for me to do.
   —I do many things well, many things right.
   —I have a lot to offer others.
2. Remind myself that:
   —Sex interest is normal.
   —With the help of the Lord, I have the power to avoid sexual activity before marriage.
   —I can be healthy and happy without a sexual outlet at this time in my life.

Reinforcement plan

1. Repeat the word *stop!* whenever I am aware of a sexually explicit thought, and turn attention to non-sex-related thinking.
2. Repeat the word *stop!* whenever I am aware of a self-critical thought.

Spiritual plan

1. Pray specifically for faith in myself.
2. Spend more time in Church meetings and in Church-related activities.
3. Pray specifically for power to control my sexual desires.

Step 3: Evaluate the Results

Assess the effectiveness of your plan, modify where necessary, and continue until the habit is under control.

Personal Power Is Possible

Lehi's words, "Men are, that they might have joy" (2 Nephi 2:25), are a reminder to us that we can be happy. Since self-direction is essential to happiness and productivity, it must also be true that we can learn to develop personal power. This book has been written to help you build greater faith in that possibility and asks to offer some concrete suggestions as to how you might develop more skill at self-direction.

Those who develop great skill in secular pursuits—Olympic athletes, for example—spend great amounts of time in practice, and the successful ones don't give up, even though their goals must look hopeless to them at times. I suppose the same can be said of those who will win "gold medals" in the celestial kingdom. They will achieve exaltation only after a lot of practice and continued faith in the possibility, even in the face of frequent failure.

Index